WHY? STUDY ABROAD IN THE USA

***

WHAT TO EXPECT AND HOW TO PREPARE!

Mike Matsuno

GoGlobal!
Fairbanks Honolulu Tokyo
Goglobal.me

Copyright © 2017 by Mike Matsuno

All rights reserved. No part of this publication may be reproduced, distributed, or transmitted in any form or by any means, including photocopying, recording, or other electronic or mechanical methods, without the prior written permission of the publisher, except in the case of brief quotations embodied in critical reviews and certain other noncommercial uses permitted by copyright law.

*To my Dad and Mom,
who always gave me the freedom, love
and wings to be me.*

TABLE OF CONTENTS

WHO is this Book For? 1
WHY was this Book Written? 2
The Beginning 3
My Study Abroad Experience 6
What is Study Abroad? 9
What Study Abroad is Not 13
Different Types of Study Abroad Programs 15
    Different Categories of Study Abroad Programs: 19
Why do you Want to Study Abroad? 21
The Global Perspective 23
Why Study Abroad in the United States? 25
Selecting a University in the US 28
Applying for Admission to US Universities 33
Financial Costs and Scholarships 38
Active Learning and Teaching in the US 44
Global Life Skills 51
Cultural Values 58
English Proficiency 61
Presentation Skills 66
Social Skills 74
Small Talk 75
Complimenting Others 79
How to Become a Good Conversationalist 84
    Know a Little About Everything 84
    Asking Questions 85
    Remembering Names 88
Why Current Events? 92
Making Friends 94
Being Positive 100
Risk Taking 102
Creativity 104
Sense of Humor 107
Motivation 111

Being Curious 114
Spontaneity and Improvisation 116
Independent Thinker 120
Sales and Persuasion 122
Appreciation 123
The Struggle 124
Managing Expectations 127
Failing and Building Confidence 129
Dealing with Change 132
Circumstances and Opportunities 135
Find Your Life Passion and Purpose 140
The Global Citizen 142
It is All Up to YOU! 145
Preparation Checklist 148
Conclusion: You Will Never Be the Same! 152
Closing Comments 156
With Sincere Appreciation 157
About the Author 158
Notes 160

WHO IS THIS BOOK FOR?

Initially, my intent for writing this book was to help guide and inform Asian students (and parents) who were interested in study abroad opportunities in the United States (US). However, after meeting a number of students from countries outside of Asia, who raised similar questions and issues regarding what to expect and how to best prepare for studies in the US, I realized the contents of this book could potentially help many other non-western foreign or international students also interested in studying in the US. This book can also benefit newly arriving immigrants into the US, as they will likely experience similar situations as the newly arriving foreign students. While many of the examples in this book stem from an Asian or Japanese perspective, I believe the basic concepts and issues may also be applied to many other countries and cultures.

If you would like more information about various universities to study at in the US or have any questions, comments or suggestions, please visit my webpage at goglobal.me

Readers of this book are also encouraged to give feedback or write a review. Your review and comments will help others know what information was most useful and important. Please also feel free to email me directly about anything regarding this book and/or study abroad opportunities in the US. I look forward to hearing from you.

Live the Dream and Go Global!

Mike Matsuno
Email: mikematsuno@mac.com
Website: Goglobal.me

WHY WAS THIS BOOK WRITTEN?

When I was a university student like many of you, I was fortunate enough to go on a one-semester study abroad program to Japan. That experience would change my life forever. I wrote this book in hopes of encouraging and inspiring young people from all over the world to think about a study abroad experience, ideally in the US. I believe that the US offers so many opportunities and the US higher education system educates foreign students about life's necessary "Global Success Skills," which I write about in this book. I also offer some suggestions that foreign students may find useful for preparing them to manage their expectations, to ensure they have a once in a lifetime, life-changing experience from the very first moment they step foot onto a US campus.

THE BEGINNING

I am an Asian American originally from Hawaii. A fourth generation (Yonsei) Japanese American, which means that my great grandparents came from Japan and immigrated to Hawaii over 120 years ago. My parents are third generation (Sansei). They do not speak any Japanese; they only speak English.

I attended Willamette University, a small liberal arts college in Salem, Oregon. When I was at Willamette, I decided that I wanted to go on a study abroad adventure in my junior year, so I applied through the study abroad organization called American Institute for Foreign Study (AIFS) to attend the University of Nairobi in Kenya, Africa.

Everyone, including my parents, thought it was crazy and told me not to go. They wanted me to go somewhere closer and safer. They suggested Japan, as Willamette had an exchange program with a sister city university called the International College of Commerce and Economics (today known as Tokyo International University). But I was stubborn and determined and I didn't want to study in Japan.

Maybe it was because I was of Japanese American heritage and I felt it was going to be too similar. At that time, I was very naive and thought that to study abroad in Japan would be boring–I was thinking what would be so different between Japan and the United States? Both countries were economically strong and modern and Japan would be just like the United States, except the people would have Japanese faces and black hair just like me.

I wanted to go to Africa, the "Continent" to experience a place that was totally different from the US where I thought I could get the "real" study abroad experience and every day would be an exciting adventure. In January of my sophomore year, I sent in my $25 application fee and waited to hear from AIFS in Washington D.C. My poor Dad and Mom, who were both very worried about the crime and social unrest in Kenya at the time, pleaded with me to change my mind. But I was strong headed and said "No." I was going to Africa to learn Swahili!

Then in April, I got a phone call from AIFS and they told me that the Kenya program had been cancelled due to not enough students enrolling. I asked them what was the minimum number of students required for the Kenya program. The AIFS staff person said that they needed six students to run the program. I was thinking that was not so many and asked, "How many students applied?" "One," she answered, "You were the only one." I got off the phone and was so disappointed. There was so much anticipation and I had told everyone that I was going to study abroad in Africa, and now I wasn't going anywhere.

But I could not return to a normal life on campus the following fall semester, it would have been too much of a letdown. As a result, I knew I had to go somewhere. And so I thought of what other study abroad programs might still be open. It was already late in the spring semester, so one of Willamette University's study abroad programs would be the best hope to still be able to go. There was a study abroad program to Costa Rica, but I didn't speak Spanish. And there was of course, Japan.

While at Willamette, I had taken two years of Japanese language courses. I also had several classmates and six from my Beta Theta Pi Fraternity who were going to Japan on this study abroad program. As a result, after giving it some thought, I decided to change my attitude about Japan and make the most out it. I applied for the study abroad program to the International College of Commerce and Economics (ICC) in Japan for one semester with the exchange group of 25 other Willamette students.

As I left the airport in Honolulu for Japan that fall semester, I had no idea what awaited me in Japan. However, from the very first moment that

THE BEGINNING

I arrived in Japan, I experienced the shock of my life as to how everything was so different, unique and unbelievable. The opportunity to study abroad would be the most powerful, life-changing experience of my life. Since that study abroad experience I have lived, studied, and worked in Japan for over 20 years. Study abroad and Japan had changed my life forever and I would never be the same again.

I have also come to realize why study abroad is so important for young people from all countries. I also observed and strongly believe that for non-English speaking foreign or international students, there is an extremely huge benefit and value to studying in the US or other western countries. That is why this book was written to encourage and help foreign or international students manage their expectations more realistically and help them prepare and maximize their study abroad experiences to the US.

MY STUDY ABROAD EXPERIENCE

Studying abroad in Japan was totally different from what I had expected. I was naive and so way off the mark. My thinking was that since I was a Japanese American and had studied two years of Japanese in college, that everything would be so similar to Hawaii and the US. I was overly confident that I would be able to communicate in Japanese and that I already knew about the Japanese culture and the way of thinking. After all, we ate a lot of Japanese food at home in Hawaii, we pounded and made mochi (Japanese rice cakes) each year, and always celebrated New Year's following many Japanese customs and traditions that were handed down from generation to generation.

Unbeknownst to me, what I thought was Japan and Japanese culture could not have been farther from the truth and reality of what Japan was really all about. My experiences in Japan were totally "mind-blowing," attempting to understand the Japanese perspective and the mindset of thousands of years of history. I had misconceptions about the culture, the behavior, the toilets, the food, and almost everything else Japanese. The only thing in Japan that was familiar was that it had McDonald's. But even the Big Mac tasted slightly different!

So, in short, nothing was the same. And no one understood my Japanese. I learned very quickly that my two years of studying the Japanese language in the US didn't even equate to a kindergarten level of Japanese. I was humbled and enlightened at the same time by my ignorance and lack of depth. It would be the one experience that would affect me in every part of my being–academically, emotionally, and mentally.

MY STUDY ABROAD EXPERIENCE

That was over 30 years ago. I have since spent over 20 years at different points of my life as a student, an intern, lodge employee, teacher, university administrator, and as a wanderer in Japan. My study abroad experience in Japan for just that one fall semester would impact my life in ways that no one could have ever imagined. That experience would teach me about cultural differences, empathy, the power of images, my perceived and actual identity, and that in the larger picture of things, being American or Japanese didn't really matter because basically we were all human beings. The universal values of kindness, love, compassion for others, and to treat people with respect and dignity were all the same to everyone in the world. It did not matter what country you came from, what your ethnicity might be, and what God you believed in.

That first study abroad experience to Japan was so powerful, that after Japan, I have participated in seven other different study abroad programs, including four other times to Japan, one to Guatemala, one to Indonesia, and one to Laos. All of these study abroad programs had different learning outcomes and purposes. I would work and save money and then study abroad in another country or participate in another study abroad program in Japan. I quickly learned that traveling as a tourist and studying abroad were totally different. Every one of my study abroad experiences have made me a better person, have given me different insights and skills, and have taught me so much about people and how to interact, speak and live with one another.

Since that first study abroad experience, I have studied in graduate schools in both the US and Japan and I have also taught as a university faculty member in both countries. I believe that I now have a very good perspective from the vantage point of being both a student and a teacher and having experienced the eastern and western educational differences of teaching and studying.

MY STUDY ABROAD EXPERIENCE

I have also worked in international education for over 25 years, first as a faculty instructor in charge of sending American exchange students from the University of Alaska Fairbanks to Japan, then as the Director of the International Center of Osaka Gakuin University, later as an international consultant in charge of recruiting and developing university partnerships in Asia for California State University Monterey Bay, and presently doing consulting for Haddington International Education (HIE) in Dublin, Ireland and working with the Japan Study Abroad Foundation (JSAF) in Tokyo, Japan.

Consequently, I have experienced the entire spectrum of working in international education on both sides of the Pacific, from understanding and institutionalizing the actual language and culture teachings, to the negotiations and development of international programs and curriculum, and finally to the marketing and recruiting of students for higher education institutions in Asia to the United States.

Through all of my life experiences, I now understand very well why study abroad is so important for university students and young people throughout the world. My life's passion is to reach out and inspire as many non-English speaking foreign or international students as possible to study in the US or other western countries. This is because I strongly believe that it would be the opportunity of a lifetime for foreign students to be exposed to such a different way of thinking, to experience the cultural and social diversity, to engage in the different methods of education and learning, to be enamored with the big and crazy ideas of "out-of-the-box" thinking, and to have the personal and academic freedoms that many have not experienced before. Moreover, the foreign students will have the opportunity to learn and live the lessons of intercultural communication, shared learning, and multicultural diversity. And even at the smallest scale, all of these lessons lead to mutual understanding and trust, which can only create a better world to live in.

WHAT IS STUDY ABROAD?

Study abroad is generally defined as studying in another country, in another culture, and for many, in a different language other than your own. But what study abroad really is–it's a life-changing experience. And if you choose to embark on this journey, all of your future decisions, goals, and ambitions will be in many ways affected. You cannot help but be profoundly engaged when you are studying abroad. You will continually be exposed to new ideas, different ways of thinking, unique experiences, and diverse people, all of which will influence and impress you in ways that no one can really imagine unless they themselves have studied abroad. Consequently, each person receives different things from studying abroad. Each experience is customized for each individual and determined by how involved you are and how much you put into the overall experience.

For many students, study abroad is an uncertain, rather lofty and vague image. Many students envision study abroad as an opportunity of meeting unique and different people from exotic lands which they had never heard about before. For others, it has a lot more to do with just having fun and great experiences more than struggle and adversity. And yet for those who understand the potential of such an experience, it is the path to a better life and successful job. No matter what images students have before they arrive in the US, most students do not really understand the true difficulties and challenges that they will face until they actually arrive at their university campus.

Study abroad is not for everyone, and for those of you who have no interest or definitely do not want to go, you should not go, even if your parents want you to go. It has to be your own decision and you have to want to go or it could end up being a very miserable, lonely, and costly experience for you and your family. Study abroad should be for those students and young people who want to experience new things, meet new people, challenge themselves, broaden their horizons, and explore self-discovery which may be the biggest lesson of all, about who they are, where they come from, what they believe in, and what they stand for.

For those of you who are not sure but part of you wants to take the risk, I would strongly encourage you to take the plunge and study abroad. The reason is if a part of you wants to go, but you end up not going, later in your life, you may regret not going and always will wonder how different your life would have been had you gone. Because without a doubt, your life would have been very different. And that regret is something that may haunt you for the rest of your life.

I am a true believer that 95% of the students who do go on a study abroad program will return satisfied and fulfilled, with new skill sets and an open mind full of possibilities for the future. Not all students will return home in awe of studying abroad, but they will still have acquired the know-how, experience, skills, language, and the sense of accomplishment that they would have never received had they remained in their home country.

Study abroad is a big risk and it can be very expensive. It could be one of the most difficult and yet most rewarding experiences there are in life. It will open your mind up to self-discovery and new ideas and the world. Moreover, you will meet so many interesting people from all over the world, not only Americans, but international students from far off places. You will make lifetime friends from all over the world whom you may visit someday and/or they will visit you.

As the saying goes, "You cannot see the forest from within the trees." This means that many times, you cannot see things while you are deeply embedded within your own culture and society. That is because at home, you are completely immersed in daily life, there is no place to step back and look at it from the outside, from another perspective. That is why, ironically, leaving your home country is the best way to learn and understand more about your country, your values, and your identity.

You will also realize the positives and the not-so-positives of your home country and of the US. Comparison is the key to improvement and to critical thinking. When you can see other ways of doing things and solving problems, it will stimulate your mind to think deeper about why things are as they are at home and in the US. And this process is important to becoming a critical thinker, and hopefully, solving future problems that will make a difference in this world.

I am from Hawaii where very few local students leave the islands and go on study abroad programs. When I ask the students of Hawaii about going on study abroad, they say that "Hawaii is the best place to live, so we don't need to go anywhere." To those students and young people who live in places like Hawaii, I tell them that while they may think that they live in the "best place in the world," they have to leave to really find out if that is really true.

For without any comparison, how can you decide that you live in the best place or the most suitable place? And what is so interesting is that once some of the Hawaii students leave their "little cocoon" in the islands and venture out on study abroad opportunities, they almost always suddenly realize the vastness and incredible adventure and excitement that exists in the world. And they too, are never the same.

Being able to study abroad could be an eclectic collection of unforgettable experiences that compels us to open and broaden our views of the world and people; it puts us in countless uncomfortable, embarrassing, and awkward situations; and it teaches us the skills to be flexible and adaptable so we can quickly pivot to different ways of thinking and behaving when necessary.

WHAT IS STUDY ABROAD?

Studying abroad teaches us the value of getting along, being a team player, and making lifetime friendships. It teaches and shows us tolerance, empathy and compassion for one another, and gives us an understanding and acceptance of people throughout the world whom we would have never met had we stayed home. I always thought that if everyone in the world had the opportunity to study abroad, the world would be much more peaceful and true world peace would actually be a possibility. It is well known that the secret to happiness is not wealth or fame, but good relationships with family and friends. It's as simple as that.

I would say that in your life, in the top five events that will be life changing for you, such as getting married, having children, etc., a study abroad experience would be one of the top five. The study abroad experience touches us in every part of our persona, not only in our minds and emotions, but all five senses of our being are sensitized and our human "antennas" are up for maximum input. And of course, study abroad will give you the language skills, the higher English language test score, and the practical job-related skills that you originally envisioned at the start of your study abroad experience.

But keep in mind that studying abroad is so much more than just the practical and physical "hard skills." It can be the one experience, the one platform, that offers you the opportunity to reach your true potential, to challenge and push yourself beyond what you believed you could do, and when it is all said and done, it will leave you with the confidence and self-esteem that no one can ever take away from you. There is nothing in life that truly comes close to such an all encompassing, life-changing experience of choice than a study abroad experience. If you are interested and want to know more–read on!

WHAT STUDY ABROAD IS NOT

Study abroad is a life-changing experience that will change you and you will never be the same. But study abroad is not for everyone and students and parents should also understand what it is not.

Unfortunately, many students and parents have no concrete idea of what study abroad is all about. Many parents think that by simply going on a study abroad experience, that miraculously their child will grow up to be an adult, attain a higher education diploma or certificate, graduate, become more fluent in the English language, acquire skills that will help them get a good job, become a global citizen, be able to work abroad or with foreigners in their home country, and other lofty expectations.

All of this could potentially be true, but it will only happen if the student is prepared for the experience and strictly applies him/herself to the challenges that will be presented throughout the many new experiences that one will encounter. Add in the fact that every student is different and what they acquire and learn and bring home varies to different degrees.

In short, study abroad is one of the most difficult challenges that an individual will experience in his/her lifetime. Not only in regards to academics, but in terms of making friends, getting along with roommates and other students, communicating with new peers, and learning social and life skills. However, the potentially greatest asset that an individual can acquire at this stage of their life will be his/her innate ability to cope and be flexible in adjusting to new circumstances as they are encountered. A person who is too young age-wise may not have the maturity, common sense, and/or the perseverance to properly adjust to handling different circumstances. Likewise, an older person may be too set or rigid in his/her ways to effectively adjust to changing situations. Nevertheless, college-age

WHAT STUDY ABROAD IS NOT

individuals are at that exciting age where they are trying to establish their identity and develop their personality to be more successful in life.

Study abroad is not a vacation or for sightseeing, although there will be many opportunities to see and experience many new places around the campus, in the local community, throughout the state, and in the US. Study abroad is usually not for students who have had emotional or mental challenges and illnesses in the past. Many parents believe that by sending their child who may have had some mental challenges at home to the US, that it will help their child to grow up and changing the environment will allow this to happen. In some cases this is true. However, in the majority of other cases, the reverse happens.

Many of the emotional and mental challenges that adolescents and young adults may have had at home will many times later appear in one form or another during the study abroad experience because the individual may not possess the necessary coping skills or emotional maturity to properly deal with the challenging social and academic situations.

Whether it is relationship or behavior issues, lack of social skills or not being able to understand or display empathy, these types of shortcomings will most likely hinder the individual's growth because challenges and struggles tend to become much more amplified in such a foreign, challenging environment. For some students, they become overwhelmed and depressed in an environment that can be extremely demanding and requires a wide range of effective life and coping skills.

One also has to remember that the foreign students will most likely have to study as much as two or three times as hard as their American classmates, as they first will have to master all four skills of English (writing, speaking, listening, and reading) and be able to convey their ideas in clear and logical English which may be very challenging. Secondly, they have to be able to comprehend, absorb and understand the class and course content. Socially, they have to be able to communicate effectively with new friends and roommates so they can make friends and establish a support network of peers.

So, it is not a good idea for parents to send their child on study abroad programs without the individual being mentally sound and strong and who can withstand a lot of different types of pressures and expectations that might be put upon them. If there is any question, visiting a psychologist or mental health professional and first getting an opinion might be the best thing if one has any doubts as to whether or not an individual is really ready to go on a study abroad experience. If a child has had serious emotional and/or mental challenges when growing up, a study abroad experience is not really the best place for them to try and find themselves.

DIFFERENT TYPES OF STUDY ABROAD PROGRAMS

Study abroad programs vary and can be defined and categorized in a number of ways. The purpose and the length of time of each program will differ. Moreover, each type of study abroad experience has its own pluses and negatives. It can be from two weeks up to four years or longer. I think what most universities consider as a long-term study abroad experience is a minimum of one or two semesters. Anything less than one semester is considered a short-term study abroad experience.

There are several levels and kinds of study abroad experiences. Some foreign students attend US universities to study the English language in ESL (English as a Second Language) programs. Although this is great as a first step, it is only the tip of the iceberg. If you study abroad for a year

DIFFERENT TYPES OF STUDY ABROAD PROGRAMS

and are in the ESL program the entire time, you will potentially have a life-changing experience but it will be a somewhat limited view of what a true study abroad program can offer to an individual.

The reason is if you look at the student makeup of the ESL classes, do you have any American classmates? No. There will be other international students who are there for the same reasons, to study and improve their English. So, ESL students will potentially have a great experience meeting and becoming acquainted with other foreign students from all over the world. But unless these students make a very conscious effort to explore and expand these experiences to include more of the typical college life with Americans, the studying abroad experience could potentially be more limited.

Although for ESL students, one's experiences may be a more limited view of what study abroad programs can potentially offer, it still will be well worth the time and effort. Usually students will study ESL for one semester or one year and then continue on into the regular university program where they will start studying subject-based courses in English. This pathway may also be a good way to gradually transition into university academics in the US, but it can take more time and, therefore, be more expensive.

The other potential trap for students who may have classmates from their home country attending the ESL program is that they will end up spending most of their time outside of class with people from their home country, speaking the home language, cooking and eating their home food, going to visit restaurants that serve their home country food, and traveling around and spending all of their time together with their fellow country people. Of course, everyday life is comfortable and very enjoyable when "hanging out" with people from one's own country. But this does

DIFFERENT TYPES OF STUDY ABROAD PROGRAMS

not help the students' English proficiencies and becomes more of a fun but more like an expensive vacation, and a huge lost opportunity.

I knew a Japanese student of mine who had gone on a study abroad program to Hawaii for one year. She returned to Japan one year later with no apparent difference or change. If anything, her spoken English had gotten worse. And why? Prior to her leaving Japan, although I had warned her very strongly several times about not staying only with other Japanese students and speaking Japanese, it fell on deaf ears.

In Hawaii, there were so many Japanese students in the ESL program that she only stayed and hung out with Japanese friends outside of ESL classes. By doing so outside of ESL classes, she spoke only Japanese, lived with another Japanese national, cooked and ate Japanese food, and did everything, including traveling and going sightseeing together with her Japanese friends. Her parents basically paid for a very expensive vacation or holiday, which barely falls into the category of a true study abroad experience, but she chose that path and "we reap what we sow."

The choices are available to every study abroad student. One gets to determine one's own destiny on study abroad programs. One gets to choose the length of the program, what one will study, how hard one will study, and who one will become friends with and "hang out" together with. All of these choices will determine your final results and what you take home when the study abroad program is completed. It is 100% a foreign student's choice and responsibility as to whether the study abroad experience was maximized or not.

To begin a study abroad program as a freshmen student and to attend a US university for four years would definitely be the best experience but potentially the most costly. Second would be those universities which allow transfers after the freshmen or sophomore years and where an individual spends two to three years on a study abroad program in the US.

DIFFERENT TYPES OF STUDY ABROAD PROGRAMS

There are foreign students that come on a 2+2 articulation program, where the students do their first two years, namely their freshmen and sophomore years, at a home country university and then do the final two years which translates to the junior and senior years at a university in the US.

Some home country universities will also issue their own degree so the student could graduate with two university degrees, one from their home country university and the other from a university in the US. Other home universities do not issue a degree for the two years of study at their institution, but they do educate and prepare the students to transfer to a four-year university in the US. These are called "American Diploma Transfer Programs" which are very popular in countries like Malaysia.

Every study abroad experience is unique and every student takes home something different. Of course, the longer the stay in the US, the more potential for a full and complete educational and study abroad experience. But every study abroad experience, even if it is only for one to two weeks, can have a big impact on students and participants. It still can have the potential to change students' thinking and futures.

I believe the ideal timeframe for a study abroad experience, if the student and/or family can financially afford it, would be for a two to four-year period. That should be sufficient time for the student to really grow and mature and to truly assimilate and understand the American people and their way of thinking. It usually takes almost one semester just to get used to the US university system, style of classroom teaching, the amount of assignments and homework, how and what to study, and, of course, becoming more comfortable and proficient with the English language used by the teachers and classmates.

DIFFERENT TYPES OF STUDY ABROAD PROGRAMS

Different categories of study abroad programs:

1) Four-year undergraduate diploma (degree seeking). Fully attend and graduate from an American college or university.
2) Transfer from home country college or university and spend 2-3 years at a US campus. The goal is to graduate with a degree from an American university/institution (degree seeking).
3) 2+2 articulation program which translates to 2 years at the home country university plus another 2 years at a US campus (degree seeking). This may sometimes result in receiving two degrees, depending on the home university requirements. Otherwise, it will be only the US degree.
4) 1-2 semesters of studying abroad with an emphasis on regular subject-based content courses in English.
5) Summer school, usually four weeks in June or July or sometimes a winter session of 3-4 weeks in January.
6) Internships, typically only a 2-4 weeks experience as a non-paid intern working in the US. This option needs to be examined more closely as to what other intern-related expenses are included or not such as housing, transportation costs, meals and/or future employment possibilities.
7) English language programs (ESL) from 1-2 semester programs or 2-4 weeks in intensive summer programs.
8) Combination programs: First semester taking ESL courses and then the second semester in regular subject-based courses.
9) Customized ESL and culture programs to increase students' English proficiency and cultural understanding, usually 2-4 weeks, with classmates from the home university in the same class.
10) A step-up type of program of first taking ESL classes, then attending summer school (1-2 regular courses), and finally in the

DIFFERENT TYPES OF STUDY ABROAD PROGRAMS

fall semester being able to enroll full-time in regular subject-based courses. All three steps are ideally taken in one calendar year.

So it is up to each individual to determine what type of study abroad program might be best suited to fit individual objectives and goals. Of course, the longer one remains on a study abroad program, the greater potential for reaping more benefits from the complete experience. To completely immerse yourself in the US and in the English-speaking world, I would recommend a two year stay, if possible, to maximize the value of studying abroad in the US.

One semester is almost too short as it takes about one semester to get used to taking regular courses in English and learning how to adapt to the American educational system of studying and learning. One year is good, but I think to get the full picture and maximize the experience, at least two years is the best. For most students, a longer experience is preferable because it tends to improve the student's English skills, academic knowledge, social and life skills, and critical thinking and processing skills. However, it may depend on what one can afford and also what is the purpose and objective to studying abroad.

For those who have the financial resources and support and who really want a serious and life-changing study abroad experience, take a risk and go to the US to get your undergraduate or graduate degree/diploma.

WHY DO YOU WANT TO STUDY ABROAD?

When I asked some Asian students this question, there were many varied answers and reasons. However, the most common reasons to go on a study abroad program were:

1) To have experiences and see things which are not possible in one's home country
2) To make friends from all over the world
3) To be able to speak English fluently
4) To get a high IELTS (International English Language Testing System) or TOEFL (Test of English as a Foreign Language) test score to get a good job
5) To acquire practical skills and knowledge that will help a person get a good job

The reasons above are all very practical and sensible. Most students and their parents associate a study abroad experience with future job opportunities. The hope is that the skills and language ability one acquires while on a study abroad program will help the individual get a good job and a descent salary at a big and well known company.

Depending on the economic level and condition of one's native country, the reasons for going on a study abroad program sometimes differ. It is related to Maslow's Hierarchy of Needs. The more affluent a country becomes, the greater the focus is on the individual for self-development, experiences, and relationships. But until a country's Gross Domestic Product (GDP) per capita passes the poverty line, the focus is generally on getting a good job and making money to move up the social ladder to a better life.

WHY DO YOU WANT TO STUDY ABROAD?

Students from countries like Japan and Korea, which are economically strong, will have a tendency to want to focus on making international friends, learning English, experiencing different things, and sightseeing in the study abroad country. However, countries which are still on the upswing of economic development usually have a more practical financial expectation which makes sense as the costs for individuals to study abroad in the US or another western country are extremely expensive.

Nevertheless, many Asian families from developing countries often collect or borrow money from relatives and friends to send their son or daughter on study abroad programs with the belief that the individual will eventually return home or work overseas somewhere with the skills, language and college degree that will help the person get a good job with a high salary. So economics does have a lot to do with it. Additionally, there is a lot of pressure on these students from developing economies to do well and graduate on time.

The above practical reasons given for study abroad are all very important. However, I hope that all students and young people will also look at study abroad opportunities from another perspective, a global perspective. The attainment of career skills and language proficiency for employment will usually come naturally from their study abroad experiences, but there is another level of thinking and soft skills sets which I call "global success skills." I hope individuals will be aware of and make a conscious effort to attain these success skills.

In my eyes, besides making friends and getting a good job, I think that all foreign students going to the US should also be made aware of other immeasurable attributes and soft skills that are perhaps as important to the individual as the hard skills and practical reasons they gave as to why they want to go on study abroad programs. I call it reaching for the global perspective.

The Global Perspective
1) A life-changing experience
2) To personally mature, develop, and grow
3) To attain intercultural competency and empathy
4) To acquire a global mindset

A life-changing experience: A study abroad experience is usually so intense that it affects an individual at all levels of one's being. Academics is only one part, the rest of the experience is made up of friendships, experiences, classroom interactions, living together, travel, sports, and daily interaction with others. Naturally, the longer you can be part of a study abroad experience, the better the chances for a more meaningful experience. I believe 2-4 years is best, but even if an individual can do one semester or one year, the experience will definitely still be very powerful. Even for those who can only afford 2-4 weeks in the summer, that is still enough to at least experience the beginning of attaining a global perspective.

Maturity, personal development and growth: Many foreign students live at home in their native country and commute to their university. For these students who live at home, the opportunity to live on one's own would be the first big step to help them to grow up and mature. The opportunity to live on one's own in the United States with roommates from the US or another country who speak another language is a huge step that will help you to grow and mature very quickly.

Some foreign students who have already experienced living in a school dormitory know the struggle of living with other roommates. Living closely with people outside of one's family can be very difficult and stressful, even if everyone speaks the same language and comes from the same culture. Imagine when you take away the common language and same cultural denominator and put two students together as roommates from two different countries. The challenges, struggles and the learning that takes place can be hugely beneficial and also extremely challenging at the same time.

But that is the exact reason why I always recommend to international students to take a double room instead of a single room, for without the struggle and challenge of learning how to actively communicate and get along with someone from another country, one will not fully acquire all the benefits of studying abroad. And as a side note, first learning to live with another person is the best kind of practice for when you get married!

Intercultural competency and empathy: This is the ability to observe and understand differences in culture and behavior and to not make rash or emotional decisions or judgments, but to be able to critically think and learn the reasons why some people behave the way they do. This also requires the ability to separate a personality trait or character flaw from a cultural norm and behavior. What study abroad will teach you is how to be culturally aware of social cues and hidden nuances.

Cultural empathy is the ability to feel and understand what someone from another country and culture is feeling or going through. In the US, the Native American Cherokee Tribe has a proverb that says, "Don't judge a man until you have walked a mile in his shoes." The proverb is saying that only after you have truly felt or experienced what another person has been through can you really understand his/her situation and adversities. That proverb embodies cultural empathy.

Global Mindset: This is really the final goal–to be able to reach a level of thinking that is visionary and wide, that you can quickly and accurately assess a situation, critically think and resolve issues, and explore or solve problems from various angles and cultural perspectives. A global mindset requires not only using a Middle Eastern or a Chinese or an American point of view, but using an eclectic array of cultural and global perspectives and mindsets to not only solve problems, but to understand how we can all get along and make the world a better place. That is the goal of the true global citizen.

WHY STUDY ABROAD IN THE UNITED STATES?

Much of what I write in this book about global success skills can also usually be applied to other western countries like the United Kingdom (UK), Canada, Australia, and New Zealand. However, please keep in mind that although there is a similar base of western culture and English, each of these English-speaking countries still retain their own character, culture, and subtle differences. But for this book, I have focused on the United States (US) because that is where I have been raised and educated, as well as I believe there is no other country in the world quite like the US. It is the world's third largest country in regards to a population of 320 million people and geographically the third largest country in physical land area. It is a very free, open, independent, progressive, and diverse country, but with distinctive regional characteristics. It is almost like having many mini-countries within a country.

It has many social problems like any other country, but America can offer an individual the tools, opportunities, and the freedom to dream and create the endless possibilities in life. I think that even with the negative aspects of the United States, regarding social issues such as gun control, inner city racial tension, drug addiction, homelessness, political divisiveness, and more, the positives for international students to study in the US, far outweigh the negatives.

WHY STUDY ABROAD IN THE UNITED STATES?

In the US, one can experience the freedom to create and think and be whomever the individual wants to be and experiment and challenge oneself to try new things that have never been attempted in one's home country. That is what America is really all about, it is truly the land of opportunity and freedom. And when you study abroad in the US, you will understand just what that means and it will be up to you to take advantage of all the opportunities around you should you choose to do so.

Please keep in mind that compared to other countries with hundreds of thousands of years of history, culture and foundation, the US is still very young and only a 240-year old experiment. Outside of the indigenous Native American Indians, the Polynesian people of Hawaii, and the Eskimos, everyone else in the US is a relatively recent immigrant from one place or another. It is one of the most diverse countries where the majority is made up of immigrants and descendants of immigrants from all over the world. You will not find another country in the world with such diversity and breadth.

In the US, it seems like you theoretically have taken different races, ethnicities, groups of people, and religions and put them into a closed tin can, shaken them around, and poured the contents out. And that is what you have in the US today. Therefore, the US is still a "work in progress" and the jury is still out on whether, long term, the US will be or not be a successful experiment.

In comparing higher education systems throughout the world, the US is the most widely acclaimed for having overall the most successful higher education system in the world. The US has 46 universities in the top-ranked 100 universities of the world. It also holds eight out of the top ten spots among recognized universities. Other countries like Britain and Australia also have some very well known and famous universities, but overall, for the pure number of universities in the US, with over 4,000 institutions of higher education, the US is said to be the best higher education system in the world.

Some international students and their parents believe that they should only attend a highly ranked or Ivy League-type of university in the US. However, I don't believe one has to study and graduate from a ranked or prestigious university in the US to get a good education. Of course, if you have the financial and academic capacity to attend any one of the eight Ivy League colleges, by all means do so, but keep in mind that the more prestigious or higher the rank of the institution, the competition for entry will also be that much more difficult. Most Ivy League schools have acceptance rates of less than 10%, which translates to less than one person getting accepted for every 10 students who apply for entry into the institution. However, there are hundreds, if not thousands, of universities in the US that are not ranked but where you can get a very solid education and life-changing study abroad experience.

Although there are many people who may argue this point, I also believe the United States to be the most progressive country in the world. If you just look at the business or technology fields, where are the new models, systems, and prototypes usually developed? Where does most of the new social media, gaming, entertainment, and multi-media ideas come from? Where is Silicon Valley located? All are from or in the United States.

Another interesting aspect of America is the pragmatism and character of the typical American. Not all of the American characteristics are always good or admired, but for the most part, Americans have a very unique character. Although this may be a generalization, Americans are often known to be very friendly, charitable, philanthropic, very logical, more prone to vocalize their feelings, original, very pragmatic, funny and crazy, and very results-oriented. Many of the typical Asian characteristics are quite different, such as being more reserved, humble, precise, meticulous, respectful, and self-controlled.

The typical character of many Americans may be very surprising and confusing, yet very eye opening for many foreign students who study in the US. Any individual interested in a study abroad experience needs to be prepared to enter a far different social, pop culture, and political environment than what they usually encountered in their home country. However, that is one of the big benefits of being able to study abroad.

SELECTING A UNIVERSITY IN THE US

The first thing you would do once you have decided to study abroad is the researching and gathering of information on US schools to help you decide where to study in the US. The US is a huge country geographically with so many different regions. For example, the northeast area, the South, the Midwest, the Pacific Northwest, California, Alaska, and Hawaii are some of the sub-regions of the US that are quite different from one another in regards to ethnicity, food, English accent, dress, cultural history and background, and social and political backgrounds.

Some foreign students may want to study in schools or live in areas where they have friends or relatives from their home country. Others may prefer a place like Hawaii, where the non-white population is 75% of the overall state population, which may be more comfortable for some in terms of not standing out as an ethnic minority. Yet, other foreign students may want to attend mainland US schools where there are very few students from their home country or region so they will have to integrate into the mainstream culture to have a full study abroad experience. It really depends on individual needs, comfort and risk levels, and what are the expectations. The key is to consider and apply to those universities that best fit the applicant's character and meet his/her expectations.

There are over 4,000 higher education institutions in the US to choose from. The institutions vary in every aspect from academic quality, costs, location, student demographics, potential opportunities, etc. Anyone interested should be proactive, look at various websites, brochures, attend US study abroad fairs in one's native country, attend and listen to presentations by US university representatives that visit the area, and try to gather as much information as one can about possible universities to attend. It is also probably the best to talk to graduates or students from one's own native country who have attended or are presently attending universities or colleges in the US.

In today's world, we are very fortunate to have access to the internet. Thirty years ago there was no internet, so foreign students interested in studying abroad in the US tended to attend colleges and universities where someone they knew from their home country had attended, and followed in their forerunner's footsteps since there was not much information available. All printed communication was done primarily through the postal mail. With access to the internet today there should be no excuse for not being well informed and having a substantial amount of information about any university or college in the US.

Most universities also have an international admissions section that an interested applicant can email directly with any questions. The US institutions can even send electronic files of their brochures and other school-related information, so everything is quick and instant. Applicants can even apply online to the majority of US institutions. One of the best sources of information about specific schools are other foreign students' blogs and social media from your country or region so that one can learn about the university campus, student services and academic life.

The main thing that I always advise students when they are looking for a university to attend is to find a university that fits their needs, their character, and offers, ideally, what they hope to get out of the study abroad experience. And this may not have anything to do with a school being ranked or not. However, some parents and foreign university professors may still have an expectation study abroad students to the US should attend a ranked or prestigious university.

Of course, that is great if that is possible, but I don't believe that just because a school is ranked that it will necessarily be a suitable fit and give the student the best experience and support to be successful in their study abroad program in the US. The focus should always be on what is best for the student. The primary emphasis should be on the schools that are known to offer the ideal environment and student support services that will encourage international students to feel comfortable, have a proven track record of assisting students with opportunities to make friends, is known to have good student academic support programs, and offer a challenging environment where the student can be academically and socially successful.

I also have talked to many university administrators from Asian universities who track their students who have done 2+2 programs, where the students study two years at the home country university and two years in the US. And so far, they have told me that they have not seen any direct correlation that a graduate from a ranked university in the US will have any more success in terms of a career and future than a graduate from a non-ranked school.

And as I have previously mentioned, most US universities and colleges offer a solid and life-changing education and study abroad experience, regardless of whether it is highly ranked or not ranked at all. It does not have to be a highly ranked or prestigious Ivy League school to attain the goals of student success, accomplishment and satisfaction.

Consequently, when an individual is deciding about which US university or college to attend, one must look at several factors. The best way would be to make a comparison chart and list the various priority categories in the order of importance. What are the most important priorities? For example, what majors are the institutions known for; the reputation, prestige, or ranking of the institution; the overall social and educational environment being a good fit for the student's temperament and personality; the affordability of the school; class size ratio of one teacher to how many students; the regional location of the institution; if there are other students from your country attending or not; is the institution located in a city or rural environment; the presence of good sports or athletic programs; access to internships and scholarships; the possibility of working on campus; an assessment of the overall academic and recreational facilities; and any other important considerations or reasons.

Make a list of the top priorities. Hopefully, there will not be more than ten priorities, but there should at least be a minimum of four or five things to take into consideration. Then list in the order of importance the different categories. The top item would be the most important to you and your family, and the bottom item would be the least important.

For illustration purposes only, using the examples previously noted above in this section, let's suppose that the order of priority determined by the student interested in going abroad are as follows: Priority #1 (affordable university costs); Priority #2 (what feels like a good fit between the institution and the student's personal traits); Priority #3 (ready access to internships and scholarships); Priority #4 (the reputation or ranking of the institution); and Priority #5 (the presence of other students from the same native country at the same institution). So, now you have a priority framework of what is the most important to the least important.

The next step would be to determine a value score for each item listed. The assignment of a numerical value is purely arbitrary, but as long as the value rule which follows are honored, the process will still work. For illustration purposes, let's assign a maximum value range of 50-41 points to Priority #1, a maximum range of 40-31 points to Priority #2, a maximum range of 30-21 points to Priority #3, a maximum range of 20-11 points to Priority #4, and a maximum range of 10-1 points to Priority #5.

The next step will be to apply your priority list (for illustration purposes only) criteria to all of the institutions under consideration. Assuming there are three institutions under consideration and let's label them as Institution A, Institution B, and Institution C. That would mean applying the same priority criteria to each institution so that a numerical value can be assigned to it and later compared to the others on the list. For example, let's say that for Priority #1, a value of 50 points is given to Institution A because it seems to be the ideal fit between the personal financial ability to cover the cost.

In doing the review of the same priority against the two remaining institutions, let's assign Institution B a value of 46 points since the relative costs seem to be more of a stretch than for Institution A and a value of 41 points for Institution C because while it may still be under consideration, the costs versus affordability issue will clearly be more difficult to sustain over the time of the study abroad program.

Then taking Priority #2 and using the same process, but with a different value range, (as reflected in the paragraph above) let's assume that Institution A gets an assigned score of 35 because a fit is perceived as not being possibly ideal, but seems to be all right. For Institution B, let's assume your assigned score is 39 points because the fit seems more ideal and for Institution C, it gets an assigned score of 31 points because it seems like the least likely to be a good fit under the circumstances. So by combining the assigned points to the first couple of steps, the cumulative totals, at this point, for each institution stands at Institution A with 85 points, Institution B also with 85 points, and Institution C trailing with 72 points.

Utilizing the same process for Priorities #3-5, let's assume that the cumulative scores for these three priorities and the institutions are: Institution A: 33 more points; Institution B: 55 more points, and Institution C: 46 additional points. When adding in the totals for Priorities #1 and #2 the totals would reflect Institution A: (85+33) 118 points; Institution B: (85 + 55) 140 points, and Institution C: (72 + 46) 118 points.

These results would tend to demonstrate that Institution B clearly seems to have the best matchup potential among the selection criteria with Institutions A and C being relatively equal. By using the process suggested here, Institution B would seem to be the best overall choice among the three institutions and the first choice for a prospective study abroad experience.

APPLYING FOR ADMISSION TO US UNIVERSITIES

After you have selected possible US universities that you would like to apply to, you must work hard on clearing their admission requirements. Most universities will require the following: primary application form, letters of recommendation, a TOEFL or IELTS test score, and high school or university (transfer) transcripts, and a minimum grade point average (GPA).

APPLYING FOR ADMISSION TO US UNIVERSITIES

When applying for admission to any US university, an applicant will first need to demonstrate that one has sufficient finances or access to financial resources to pay for the anticipated costs of university tuition, housing and meals, health insurance, books, and miscellaneous personal expenses. Next, one will need a high enough TOEFL (Test Of English as a Foreign Language) or IELTS (International English Language Testing System) English test score that meets the minimum admission requirement score of the university. And third, one will need to meet the minimum GPA requirement.

Depending on the university, the required financial amount differs in order to be eligible for a student visa. For example, on the lower end for some universities, the required amount for a financial affidavit is about $28,000-$36,000 for a one year program. The actual amount will depend on the length of time you will study and your visa status at the university. An individual will have to show proof for the issuance of a Certificate of Eligibility (1-20 Form) when one applies for the student visa.

The TOEFL and IELTS tests both measure a prospective student's English proficiency and most US universities will accept either one of these test scores. The TOEFL was developed in the US at Stanford University and the IELTS was developed in the UK at Cambridge. As a special note, please be sure to check the different prospective university websites because some US institutions might only accept the TOEFL. Both tests are quite expensive to take, but you can take the tests as many times as you can afford to and that is offered in one's home country.

The TOEFL iBT test is based on a scoring range of 1-120, with 120 being the highest. The IELTS test has a range of 1-9, with 9 being the highest. In the past, the TOEFL was the main English exam used for study abroad to the US, but recently the IELTS is being offered throughout the world and is gaining more popularity in the US. Presently about 3,000 out of the 4,000 US universities accept the IELTS which is being accepted by more and more US universities. Many teachers and students believe that the IELTS is a better test which evaluates the four English skills (writing, speaking, listening, and reading) more comprehensively and fairly than the TOEFL. Today, outside of the US, the IELTS English language test is the most popular English test in the world for higher education and immigration.

The grade point average is the GPA requirement. Depending if you are a high school graduate or a college transfer student, the GPA requirement is different. The US GPA system is based on a ranking of letter grades A-F, with A being the highest and which then corresponds to number points which translates to a range of 0-4, with four being the highest: A=4, B=3, C=2, D=1 and F=0. A 4.0 GPA is the highest possible score.

To apply to the US, if your high school or university uses a different grading system other than the A-F, 4.0 GPA system, you must convert the grading system to the US GPA grading system. Sometimes the conversion of grades and scores can be slightly off, so one will need to contact the international admissions office at the prospective universities one is applying to find out the correct way to covert the home school grades to the US GPA grading system.

Depending on the US university, the GPA entrance requirement can vary significantly. For example, some institutions may be willing to accept prospective students with a GPA as low as 2.4 or 2.5 for high school graduates and 2.0 for transfer students. Other highly ranked universities may require a minimum of a 3.5-4.0 GPA to be accepted.

Required entrance TOEFL and IELTS scores can range from TOEFL iBt 61-80 and IELTS scores of 5.5-8, depending on the university. Some well known or ranked American universities have much higher GPA and TOEFL/IELTS requirements, so interested applicants will have to check on the institution's website or look at the institution's brochure for admission requirements. Some may even indicate that they don't require an English language test score, but since an individual will still have to prove that one is proficient in the English language, it would probably just be easier to send in the TOEFL or IELTS score if they meet the minimum admission requirement.

Transfer students are students who attend at least one semester at a home country university or college and then apply to enroll in a US university. So, if one intends to attend a university or college in your home country for at least one semester, although some institutions require a minimum of a year or 30 credits, there is always the option of then applying to US universities as a transfer student. The requirements are similar to high school graduates, but the GPA from the home university or college will usually replace or have to be sent in along with the high school GPA requirement. And the credits for the classes taken in the home country may be transferred to the US institution for credit if the US school accepts the course and credits. But individuals will have to send in and manage the credit transfer on their own by having the syllabi and course descriptions of the classes that have been taken translated into English and sent in to the respective US higher education institution's office which handles transfer credits from overseas applicants.

For degree-seeking students, please plan for the fact that this credit transfer process will take quite a bit of time, possibly up to six months or more. As a result, very often many transfer students will start their studies at the US university without first knowing exactly what courses taken at the home country's institution can be transferred for credit to the US university. Please also note that there are some US schools which do not have the staffing expertise to evaluate foreign university credentials or courses and for these schools you must send your transcripts to a professional credential evaluation company and have them look over your transcripts and verify your credentials. You must pay for this service and after they are completed verifying your credentials and coursework, they will usually send it directly to the US university. One example of a company who does foreign credential evaluations is World Education Services, WES at http://www.wes.org/students/.

Once a prospective study abroad student has met the initial admission requirements for a school that they are interested in applying for, the student (and possibly his/her parents) should begin to explore what other universities they may want to apply to. And that is because even if you pass the minimum admission requirements, you could still be turned down. Admissions people, depending on the school, many times look for something extra, possibly a student who can contribute something to the campus, as well as being a good academic student. Many Ivy League schools are looking more for all-around, well-balanced students, not only a high GPA or test score.

Please note the reference to "universities" rather than just a single institution. That is because entry into colleges and universities in the US is a very competitive process. There are far more American students interested in attending higher education institutions than there are available enrollment spaces for them, let alone enrollment space for interested students from outside of the country. That is why it is advisable to explore and pursue several possible options because the university or college which an applicant is most interested in may not accept the applicant for a variety of reasons. I would suggest applying to at least five US universities. Although you must pay the application fee for each university, you will keep all options open in the event that your top choices do not accept you.

If one limits their options and they don't get accepted into the school they apply to, they will have to wait another semester or another academic year to apply again in the application cycle. The reverse is also true. There are many students who apply and are accepted to more than one or two of the schools they applied to. There is nothing wrong or frowned upon in the US about submitting multiple college admission applications. It is standard practice among most students and it gives you a lot more options.

In addition to the minimum admission standards that every institution requires, an acceptance to be admitted sometimes come down to additional considerations. For example, one institution, in addition to the admission requirements, may give greater weight to applicants who have demonstrated experiences in public service or volunteer work while another school may be interested in a more well-rounded student who was active in sports, student government, and/or other extracurricular activities.

FINANCIAL COSTS AND SCHOLARSHIPS

Compared to an individual's home country, a degree/diploma seeking study abroad program tuition and housing/meal costs in the US will be much higher and costly. One should expect the typical study abroad (degree seeking) costs to be in the range of $35,000-$70,000+ (US dollar) per year, which includes tuition, housing, health insurance, books, and meal costs. Please keep in mind that this does not include additional money for personal out-of-pocket expenses. These costs are for regular degree seeking students, not exchange students or students who attend study abroad programs for only 1-2 semesters in the US where their costs will be much less than what is quoted above.

FINANCIAL COSTS AND SCHOLARSHIPS

Within the US, study abroad costs can differ and will vary significantly based on a number of variables such as the state where the institution is located, a more urban or rural environment, and whether it is a state, public, or private college or university. It also makes a difference if the institution is nationally ranked. Schools that have a good reputation such as Ivy League institutions are much more expensive. Students are paying for the brand, reputation, and prestige of studying at these Ivy League-types of institutions.

There are over 4,000 higher education institutions in the US including two-year community colleges, four-year universities, graduate schools, law schools, Master of Business Administration (MBA) schools/programs, and Ph.D. programs which offer a wide variety of costs and choices. Be sure to look carefully when viewing US university websites. Make sure the costs you see are specifically for international students because tuition costs for international students are usually two or three times higher than for domestic students or in-state students. Some private universities will offer the same tuition costs to both domestic and international students. But the overall tuition and housing/meal costs will be relatively high.

Additional financial considerations to keep in mind also include consideration of two-year and vocational colleges whose tuition is relatively cheaper than four-year universities and colleges. And some international students like to start at community colleges and transfer after two years of undergraduate work to four-year universities. The challenge here is that usually community colleges were established for American students to learn a trade or vocational skill or study for their first two years at the community college, but then transfer to a four-year university for their junior and senior years.

Since the focus was on local students, sometimes the international student support in regards to housing and academic advising for international students was not that strong at community colleges. However, recently there are some community colleges which do market strongly to foreign students and in these cases, the international student support is quite strong.

Many state community colleges have the 2+2 type programs that will allow foreign students who graduate with the community college's 2-year associate's degree to automatically be accepted into their state system's four-year university where they can complete their junior and senior years for their four-year degree.

If you want to change out of that state university system or want to attend a different university after two years, it will mean that you will need to go through the application procedure again and be accepted to another four-year college to transfer to, which most likely means having to relocate to another location perhaps in another state or city and starting all over again in terms of making friends, readjusting to different academic schedules and standards, and having to acclimatize to a new unfamiliar college campus, teaching faculty, students, and surrounding community. It is neither a good or bad thing but just one more step to be aware of and deal with.

For foreign students, the biggest factor to consider is financial costs, which naturally results in many foreign students applying to US institutions that offer scholarships to international students. There are some schools in the US that will offer certain incentives and scholarships for students who have a high GPA in high school. And some of these universities will continue the scholarship if the student maintains the required GPA while studying at the US university or college.

Financial assistance/aid in the form of scholarships, loans, or work study for international students are sometimes offered and it is many times also a part of a marketing strategy for many US schools to try and

FINANCIAL COSTS AND SCHOLARSHIPS

recruit international students. Some US schools will offer individuals scholarships that range from $500-$15,000 annually. Some will even use the phrase "50% off tuition-scholarship for international students."

But one should be very careful and if costs are a main factor then a prospective student must always look at the "fine print" which defines eligibility and/or retention requirements and the final bottom line. What is the actual tuition costs after the scholarship or financial assistance is deducted? One should always compare the bottom line tuition costs to other universities' tuition bottom line costs.

What I mean is that there are some universities which offer higher scholarships, up to 50% off their tuition, but you should also look at what the actual tuition costs are for that university. Usually those universities that offer a very high scholarship will be private universities, with a very high tuition, probably $40,000-$60,000. So even if one is offered 50% off, an individual can still pay $20,000-$30,000 a year for tuition only.

A state university's tuition may be closer to $15,000-$27,000, so if one looks at the final bottom line, the state university's tuition will still be cheaper even without any scholarship offered. So one really has to look closely at the tuition bottom line after the scholarship or financial assistance is deducted. And you also have to be careful and check if that 50% scholarship or financial assistance is only for the first year or does it continue every semester until you graduate and if there are certain stipulations that you need to do to keep the scholarship, like a minimum GPA.

Another marketing strategy of some universities which can confuse international applicants is that the brochures and websites may show only the tuition costs for one semester while most universities will usually show the full year's tuition costs (2 semesters). So at first, an interested applicant may be happily surprised at the reasonable tuition costs, only to later find out that the noted tuition was only for one semester while the other university's tuition costs were quoted for two semesters.

One more thing to be aware of is that some US universities will quote you a tuition fee that is for 12 credits per semester for an undergraduate program, which is the minimum number of credits that you need to take to be considered full time and to keep your student visa. What is not said is that you will realistically need to take 15 credits a semester if you are to graduate on time in four years. 120 credits is usually the total number of credits needed to graduate, so if you attend four years, you will need to average 15 credits per semester. But if you take 15 credits a semester, you must pay separately for the additional three credits a semester. So, also calculate the additional three credit costs into the overall costs per year. You could also take courses in summer school to make up the difference in credits, and some schools will even offer summer school courses/credits at a discounted or an in-state rate, but you still will have to factor in that you will need to pay for room and board to attend summer school. So you will have to do the comparison and decide what would be better or easier to make up the difference in credits.

Also be aware that all brochures and websites have a clause that says tuition or costs are "subject to change." This basically means that the tuition or costs that are quoted may change after the printing of the brochures. The best up-to-date information is usually on the university's website. But either way, be sure that you reconfirm directly with the international admissions people what the tuition and housing and meals costs are for the semester or year that you are applying for.

There are also a few US state universities which offer international students the same in-state tuition costs as domestic students. But usually these universities or colleges will be in locations or states that are not well known or do not have easy access to urban cities and airports for international students. But from strictly a cost standpoint, these universities will be the most affordable.

As they say in America, "You only get what you pay for," which usually means that nothing is really free. For instance, while a certain higher education program may be much cheaper, it may be because its physical location is not very attractive and/or more inaccessible or the faculty might not be very well compensated or the facilities may be lacking in many things which a more costly institution may have. So sometimes a student may have to stretch beyond the bottom line to ensure that the study abroad experiences offer the best opportunity for future success.

Saving some money on the front end may seem to be a wise investment, but there are usually potential tradeoffs somewhere in the equation. There is no point of going to study abroad if one later ends up having many regrets, especially if the experiences do not end up meeting the original goals and expectations. So, be very thorough when checking out different universities and comparing them to one another.

Also be careful whether the costs one is looking at are for "tuition only" or if the price quoted includes housing and meal plans. Some universities will give students the entire package costs, which really is the most helpful, while others, to make their costs seem lower, will give information of the tuition costs separate from the housing and meal plan costs. So, an individual needs to look at the "fine print" to compare apples with apples and not apples to cabbages.

By checking into and comparing the schools' listed information with other schools, one can better decide on what exactly the costs cover, including whether it will be for one semester or two, for tuition only or if it includes housing and meal plans, etc. So, be very careful when reading through various universities' websites and brochures.

Remember the universities or colleges are trying to market and advertise in a way to promote and sell their school. They are not trying to deceive or fool anyone, but they are using marketing strategies to try and get more students to attend their school. So, they will sometimes make things look or seem better than what they really are. One should keep in mind, in these instances, the very old saying that "When something sounds too good to be true, it probably is."

Finally, prospective study abroad students should also look at the housing/dormitory and meal plan fees. In some states and locations, due to the higher costs of living, housing and meals plan costs will be more expensive. Also compared to the universities located in urban city areas, the universities located out in the country or in more rural areas will many times have lower housing and meal plan costs. For example, if you are studying in New York City, you can naturally expect that the housing and meal plan cost will be much higher than a university in Fargo, North Dakota which may be more remote with lower costs of living and not be very well known.

ACTIVE LEARNING AND TEACHING IN THE US

In the US, college students are always encouraged to take responsibility for their own learning–to be an active learner. This generally translates to being engaged in classes with teachers and classmates and actively asking questions and participating in class discussions. Participating in classes and having an opinion is very important in the US. Many MBA classes in the US have participation in class as a large percentage of its grade.

Active learning requires a two-way exchange of information. This is in contrast to passive learning, which is more typical in Asian cultures, where a student does not actively engage in discussions and is expected to sit back passively as the information is presented in a one-way direction from the teacher to the student.

Having and sharing an opinion is really important in the US. In class, if a student is asked what does he/she think about some issue or topic and answers "I don't know," it often would not leave a good impression with the teacher or other classmates. It would give the impression that either the student wasn't paying attention, doesn't care or he/she is not intelligent enough to say something meaningful. A very "diplomatic" or vague answer is probably better than an "I don't know" answer and will temporarily be accepted at face value. Making an effort will be preferable to saying "I don't know." However, responding with an incorrect answer all the time is also not appropriate either and so you will have to exercise common sense when responding to questions in class.

In the US, students are responsible for their grades and their GPA (grade point average) is very important for scholarships, getting internships, and securing future employment. Teachers are also usually very accessible and students can ask teachers about a score or grade on a test, letter of recommendations for scholarships/jobs, or pursue issues related to a student's performance in class. Tests, quizzes, and papers are always handed back to students a few days after students have handed them in so students have quick feedback on the extent of their learning as to what they got correct or what they might have missed and gotten wrong.

This is another indication of active teaching and learning that generally takes place in the US–a continuous two-way interaction between teachers and students. This is what an American education experience is really about and definitely a different approach to what students usually experience in other cultures, especially in Asian countries.

In many Asian universities, the United Kingdom (UK), and Australian universities, the grade for a class is often based on one final exam and usually the students are not handed back their final exams. Consequently, they never really know what they answered correctly or incorrectly. A grade could be totally arbitrary and the teacher could give a student whatever grade he/she decides upon. There is also no real recourse for students to argue or contest any grade because they never get the final exam back. After report card grades come out, in most Asian universities, it is almost impossible to contest a grade or argue with a professor to change a grade.

As a result, students tend to become conditioned that once the exam is over, there is no real reason to care or worry about what you learned in the class or what grade you earned. Moreover, the GPA at many foreign universities doesn't really matter very much as it does in the US. For example, in terms of possible employment in Japan, employers are only concerned about the reputation of the university you graduated from, not your GPA.

In Japan, the GPA also has little affect on graduation. Outside of not going to classes or failing classes with an F grade, you could graduate with a GPA of 1.0, which would mean that you could technically get Ds in every class and still graduate. This would never happen in the US. A 2.0 GPA is usually the minimum required to maintain continued eligibility to graduate in the US but it is considered reflective of a very low performance.

In the US, acquired knowledge is often equated with grades and your GPA is very important when applying and competing for jobs, scholarships, and internships. The most important thing that prospective employers look for on a university graduate's application is not the status or reputation of the university you graduated from, but one's overall university GPA. However, needless to say, if you went to Harvard or an Ivy League school in the US, that would attract extra attention to some degree, but if your GPA was very low, it would not make a graduate look good because a GPA in America is a reflection of a student's knowledge and perseverance of the subject content and a reflection of one's standing in competing against other classmates at the same institution. It is the most important measurement from the university to show an individual's achievement compared to other potential job applicants.

In the US classrooms, there are constant assessments where students are graded all throughout the semester with quizzes, papers, presentations, midterm exams, and final exams. The percentages of the final grade are usually divided out among the assignments and tests, participation and attendance, and midterms and final exams. This grading system differs greatly from most Asian, United Kingdom, and Australian universities where the final exam represents close to or the entire weight of the course.

All the information about grading percentages, acceptable classroom behaviors, and rules are written on the syllabus which is handed out on the first day of class. In the US, the syllabus is similar to a form of a contract. It states what the teacher/professor expects from the students and will provide to the students during the semester. It also manages students' expectations of what they should expect to cover and complete during the course.

That is generally what students learn in the first class session in addition to how the class grade for the course will be determined. So, if students do not like the teacher's grading structure or the teacher, unless it is a required course and there is only one teacher teaching it, students may have the option to drop the class and take another class instead. Each institution's rules may differ, so students should familiarize themselves with what is permissible or not permitted as to course procedures or protocols. The ease or difficulty of the class, the grading structure, the character of the teacher are all shared and talked about by students who previously had the class and teacher. Consequently, if you are wondering who is a good teacher, it may be prudent to ask your dormmates and friends, but also be sensitive to the reliability of the source. They, however, can still be a very good source of information.

But I want to clarify something. The words "good teacher" or "good class," could potentially mean different things to different students. For example, to some students, "good teacher" or "good class" means the class is easy and it is easy to get a good grade. My definition of a "good teacher/class" is very different and is just the opposite. From my perspective, a "good teacher" was someone who really cared about the students, lectured in a very interesting and engaging way, and most of the time was a very hard grader.

I remember my two favorite professors when I was an undergraduate at Willamette University, Dr. Sue Leeson and Professor Harry Rorman. I got my lowest grades from both professors, a C+ from Dr. Leeson and a B- from Professor Rorman. But they inspired me and in every class, they lectured in a very stimulating and engaging manner, and there was no Power Point or computer presentations in those days, just chalk and a chalkboard.

But their tests and their grading were very difficult and strict. Very few students got A's in their courses and their tough reputations were well known on campus. If you were not going to attend every class and invest a lot of study time for their classes, you would not take their courses.

I don't really remember most of the professors who I received A's from and who were easy graders. So it really depends on what is your definition of a "good teacher." My advice is if you have a choice, select teachers/professors who lecture in an engaging and interesting way, are passionate about the subject they teach, and who will challenge and push you to reach your full potential. The grades are not the priority if you really want to learn and grow. Every time when you leave the class, you should know exactly what your "take home" value of the class was. This means that you clearly know what you just learned in that class.

What I really respect about the US higher education system is that it holds faculty and instructors accountable to students. Teachers have to return all assignments, quizzes, tests, and papers back to their students. This also includes final papers and final exams. Teaching faculty have to return the final exams/papers to the students or at least offer the students the opportunity to look over their final exam and score prior to when teachers hand in the grades for the course report cards. Students can even ask about an answer or grade on a test if they feel that the teacher incorrectly graded something. This allows the student to learn and understand what was correct and incorrect on the final exam. This is the strength of the US higher education system. Students are given the opportunity to review the corrected final exam and, as a result, they can evaluate what they really retained and learned over the entire semester. The review of the final exam can help the student understand what he/she did not understand or was mistaken about. And this is all done before the final grades are sent in to the academic office to be put on the course report cards. This is one main difference that separates the US higher education teaching from the UK and Australia.

I think the US higher education system is the most successful in regards to student learning because of this system of mutual accountability and review before the grades are handed in. This is what I believe that true education and active learning is all about. More than learning and memorizing the content of the subject matter, students in the US are learning "how to learn," and that is a founding principle of education.

Faculty/instructors also have actual office hours where they are physically present and are required to keep their doors open for student conferences. Conversely, students are expected to visit their offices for clarification, advice, and sometimes counseling, as needed. The US education system is very student-centered and there is much responsibility and accountability for teachers, as well as students. Teaching in the US requires a lot more work and commitment, especially when compared to other foreign universities. And this constant assessment and mutual accountability system is probably why the US is known to have the most comprehensive and best higher education system in the world.

I also think that sometimes in some countries, there is more of a focus on the "act of studying," which translates into emphasizing the individual time and effort put into the act of studying. This tends to contribute to the belief that the greater the effort of studying, the better one will do. While there is nothing wrong with having good study skills, just effort alone will not necessarily mean greater content mastery.

In the US, there is a much stronger focus on the actual learning or acquisition of insight more than the act of studying. From the time children are in primary school, parents are always asking their children daily, "What did you learn in school today?" The emphasis is always on the learning, not the act of studying. This is a big difference between the US and many other countries.

For example, the Japanese way of looking at education seems to focus more on the "effort" expended in studying. Whereas in the US, the focus is more on the learning and the results. And I think this is part of the pragmatic American mindset which is more results-driven compared to the Japanese emphasis on effort, form, and time spent studying. As I mentioned earlier, the question that I would ask myself after a university class lecture would be, "What was the take home value from today's class?"

It is not about what the professor or teacher knew or explained to you in class. The more crucial question is what did you, the student, learn from the lecture or lesson.

I will conclude this section with a quick summary of the general differences between the US universities and the United Kingdom (UK) and Australia universities. First, it normally takes four years in the US to complete enough credits for a bachelor's degree, while it usually takes only three years in the UK and Australia. Secondly, the US style of classroom teaching is much more practical, interactive and involved compared to a more theoretical based and lecture style in the UK and Australia (and Asia).

The US system also stresses more about knowing something about a broad range of things, a more liberal arts approach, whereas the UK, Australia, and most Asian systems place more emphasis on depth in one's major and area of study. And lastly, the courses at US higher education institutions emphasize much more constant assessment and engagement, whereas the majority of the UK, Australian, and Asian courses have very few class assignments if any and all or most of the weight of the course grade are determined by the final exam.

GLOBAL LIFE SKILLS

I have a good friend, Sammy Takahashi, who was originally from Japan and 30 years ago he moved to live and work in Canada. In Vancouver, he owned an English language school for many years where he could observe and understand the needs of the Asian and Japanese students who came to study English at his school.

Every year, Sammy would visit Japan to give presentations to different universities about what skills and abilities he thought the Japanese students needed to have a more global mindset so they would be more employable and successful in life. These same skills, I believe, could be applicable and relevant to many foreign students. Sammy called these essential qualities and skills the "global life skills." Below is the list of these global life skills. Sammy taught me the first four, and I added number five based on my experiences.

Global Life Skills
1) Critical and logical thinking
2) Problem Solving
3) Leadership
4) Assertiveness
5) Active communication and listening

In the US, students usually learn and acquire the global life skills throughout their studies in the K-12 (Kindergarten–12th grade) education system. Teachers at all levels create assignments and exercises that try to encourage students to think critically and be good problem solvers. They also encourage students to think independently and freely and to not just easily believe everything that is read or heard. The teacher's mantra is, "You have to be able to think for yourself!"

Critical and logical thinking is the ability of someone who can skillfully observe and assess a situation by looking at the various perspectives and coming to a logical and reasonable solution. This is an essential skill to figure out how things could be positively changed and improved. Entrepreneurs need to have this skill to be successful. Someone who has this ability is able to look at the entire picture and connect all of the dots by understanding how the different parts can fit together and work more effectively.

Critical thinking is not often taught in the general education systems of K-12 instruction in Asia/Japan and many other countries and very minimally at the university level. Outside of international schools, most of the teaching and learning styles in Asia and some other foreign universities are based on rote memory and more of a Confucian way of teaching and lecturing. The premise is that the teacher holds the wisdom and knowledge and the students should obediently listen to the lectures and take notes, receiving the wisdom of their teacher.

The students then memorize and reproduce the information/knowledge from the lecture on the tests. The classroom teaching in Asia is usually a one-way process–from teacher to student with very little if any interaction between teacher and students and no questions are asked in class. Even if the instructor at the Asian university asks the class if there are any questions, he/she is not really asking for questions. It is more like saying "See you at the next class" because students are not expected to ask any questions in class.

In the US, critical and logical thinking are embedded within the educational system. The goal is to have students think and critically look at problems and issues. There may be some classes where some teachers and professors still may use more of a rote memory approach and teaching method, but they are in the minority as the focus of US education is to create and instill independent and critical thinking. And I believe this is the big difference in philosophy between teaching and learning in the US and in Asia.

In general, Asia/Japan tends to focus on creating and raising individuals to be good citizens who obediently follow the rules, do what they are told to do, and respect authority. On the other hand, the US education system tends to focus on creating independent thinkers who can ask "why?" and who can go out into the world to be entrepreneurs, astronauts or teachers, or whatever one chooses to be. I am not saying which system is right or wrong, but it is important to recognize and understand what the main emphasis of the education system and teaching tends to be.

This is a big reason when Asian students first arrive in the US, they are often very surprised at the way American students ask questions, argue, and speak out in classes. Often, Asian students may be taken aback at how interactive and engaging the US classrooms are between the teacher and the students, as well as student to student. In some classes, the teacher is more like a coach or facilitator than a typical college professor.

Sometimes there are even too many student questions asked in class to the point that the teacher must stop the questions and discussion because he/she cannot otherwise effectively continue with the contemplated lesson/lecture. However, the sharing of ideas and the challenging of others' opinions based on logic, reasoning and emotion is the ideal of what American education is really all about. Critical and logical thinking are at the top of the global life skills list because they are the most important skills if one wants to be more engaged, employable, and successful in the world today.

Problem Solving is related to critical thinking, the ability to look at a problem from various angles and quickly figure out logically and objectively the best way to address a problem. It takes a certain kind of thinking to be a problem solver. Many people are very intelligent and may have very high test scores, but they may not be good problem solvers. Teaching students to be good problem solvers requires a different way of teaching, learning, and looking at things. It requires a different way of educating and interacting with students.

Many times, a problem solver has to use a different part of the brain. Most Intelligence Quotient (IQ) scores are based on the dependence of the left side of the brain which is more oriented to logical, concise, and detailed-oriented functions. But many times, problem solving requires the use of the right side of the brain which is more oriented to being creative, unconventional and imaginative. The ideal is always to become a whole brain person where there is an even balance of both right and left sides of the brain.

Studying abroad in the US or a western country is one of the best ways for foreign students to explore this way of thinking and training. A good example of people who are problem solvers and use both sides of their brain are the guest speakers on the Ted Talks videos on You Tube on the internet. There are thousands of Ted Talk videos sharing new, unique ideas and suggestions on possible options and solutions for personal, daily, and world problems. The Ted Talks have been taking place for over 30 years and most of the suggested ideas are from the US because of the innovative environment that requires critical thinking and problem solving skills.

Leadership styles are very different when comparing the east to the west. The western leader tends to be much more dynamic, eloquent and talented at public speaking and doing presentations, and tends to have better overall people skills. He/she also usually has a very direct and straightforward way of explaining or introducing his/her ideas and thought processes to the public. Part of this directness is also linguistic-based.

English is a very direct and "to-the-point" language–where words matter. English language speakers tend to use words to convey their ideas directly. In the US, the intention is to be direct and as clear as possible. The communication style of the US is one that displays confidence and there are much bigger gestures and hand movements, as well as gentle touches when welcoming guests which tend to show hospitality and caring.

In Asia, the way of speaking and leading are often structured to be more indirect and also to display modesty. The Asian leader is usually more humble and doesn't usually exhibit such a confident and assertive persona. In addition, Asian leaders usually will not have such large hand movement or gestures when they speak and will usually not touch or display gestures of affection when they meet someone for the first time.

Assertiveness: As previously mentioned, Asian and some other cultures tend to be more reserved and indirect. Of course, depending on which Asian country one comes from, it may vary. But in comparison to American and other western students, Asian students tend to be more on the reserved or passive side. In the US, Asian and other foreign students will need to make an effort to speak out and be more assertive. If not, people may not pay attention to them.

Ironically, many white, Caucasian foreigners, who live in countries in Asia are usually treated very well and/or given extra attention and help by the local people. As part of this expectation of reciprocity, it is only natural for Asian students to assume that when they go to the US, Americans would do the same and be very mindful and helpful to them as foreigners. But this is usually not the case. You will be treated the same as everyone else. In the US, if Asian students don't assertively speak out, they may not get any attention or help. They may just be left alone or ignored. Obviously, there are exceptions, but it would be better to prepare yourself for people who may not behave the same way as you might have expected them to treat a foreigner in their home country. By keeping this in mind, study abroad students need to be more assertive and skillfully speak out in the US or they may not get things done in a timely and efficient manner.

Active Communication and Listening: I also advise Asian students going to the US that they need to be active communicators and listeners. They should always give some kind of signal or gesture when they are

GLOBAL LIFE SKILLS

listening to someone, be it a nod, a word like "uh-huh," or some expression like "Wow, I didn't know that," or something similar, but appropriate for the situation. The Japanese have a word for this constant acknowledgement to the speaker. They call it "aizuchi" and older Japanese use "aizuchi" in the Japanese language much more than Americans do in English. But for whatever reason, maybe it is showing respect or they are in awe, but many Asian students tend to not use much "aizuchi" when conversing in English.

One has to always be engaged in the conversation, even as a listener. If an individual does not have any "affect," people will think that one is not listening, doesn't understand what is being said, or not interested in what others have to say. Worse yet, it could be misinterpreted as the individual not caring enough about what is being said or just plainly being rude. One should not be looking at his/her cell phone, texting, or listening to music while talking to someone. To do so would be thought of as displaying rude or disinterested behavior, regardless of the cultural environment. So be ready to be an active communicator and listener in the US.

Nevertheless, don't expect that all Americans will be active communicators. There are always exceptions in any culture so please keep in mind that there will be some exceptions. Some Americans might not behave well as engaged communicators as I have previously described in this section and they themselves may seem quite rude. However, keep in mind that they are on home territory and are native English speakers so they can get by without having to always be so attentive.

But as a foreign student studying in the US, one should be prepared to assert himself/herself and speak out and ask questions to get help. Americans are generally helpful if asked, so don't miss an opportunity for them to help you out. Behaving in the same way which might be acceptable in one's home country will not always work for foreign students studying in the US. Throughout the rest of the book, I will use the term "global success skills," which I use as a term that incorporates the "global life skills" as well as all the other "soft skills" discussed in this book.

CULTURAL VALUES

Every country and region has a different value system. Asian values and American/western values are quite different. So, it is only natural that there will be misunderstandings and different expectations between the eastern and western cultures. What is looked as respectful or highly valued in one culture may not be perceived in the same way in another culture. And that is why learning intercultural competency and empathy is so important.

If an individual knows what values are important to others and where they are coming from, then when others say or do something which may seem strange or rude, one will have the depth and knowledge base to understand their point of view and make the necessary paradigm shift. Here are some general values and norms that may be associated with Asian and eastern cultures:

1) Hierarchy/Seniority
2) Confucianism
3) Traditional
4) Conservative
5) Indirect communication style
6) Group-oriented
7) The presentation/outward appearance being most important
8) Saving face
9) Emphasis on non-verbal behaviors
10) Perseverance

These are just some general Asian/eastern values that are usually associated with Asian/eastern cultures and countries. Of course, we cannot associate all of these values with all people and countries from Asia. But what can be said is that there tends to be common groupings or practices of Asian values that reflect a large part of Asian behavior, culture and norms. The list noted above is just to give you a general idea of what an Asian student's base and foundation may be created from.

If you look at the US and western cultures, their general values or norms may be:

1) The individual before the group
2) Emphasis on preference for a flatter organization (rather than a hierarchical bureaucracy)
3) More informal and friendly behaviors
4) Generally more progressive orientation and values (especially in larger urban environments located on the eastern and western coasts of the US)
5) Direct communication style
6) Emphasis upon results based and outcomes
7) Emphasis on the verbal

So regardless of cultural orientation, if an individual looks at both lists, I think he/she can better understand why there could be misunderstandings or differences of perspectives when an Asian person meets a western person for the first time. Many of the values and norms seem to be oftentimes contrary. And that is why one has to be observant, ask a lot of questions, figure out where the other person may be coming from, and be mindful and open to others and their points of view and perspectives. When in doubt in a foreign environment, the saying "When in Rome, do as the Romans do" can serve as a useful guide for most unfamiliar situations.

Here are some other noted cultural differences between eastern and western cultures:
1) Emphasis upon details vs "the big picture"
2) Following tradition vs being creative
3) Safety/stability vs calculated risk taking
4) Recognized authority vs personal autonomy
5) Emphasis upon effort vs being results-driven
6) Emphasis on the rules vs being flexible

It is important to keep in mind that what is very important or valued in one culture, may not be in another. And much like a chameleon, we must learn to adapt to different environments and situations and to be more understanding and open to different points of views and ways of thinking. It is difficult not to make some judgment on a behavior or custom which we may have never seen before or what is not usually accepted as "normal" in our home country. But this is where intercultural acceptance and empathy is necessary so that an individual has the ability to literally walk in another person's shoes.

It is especially crucial for study abroad students to be flexible and open to trying and seeing things from the other person's perspective because it is all part of the learning process of being able to survive and thrive in a foreign culture. Study abroad students have the benefit of being able to experience multiple cultures and values before deciding for themselves which cultural values might be preferable for different situations that they will encounter. Pity the poor individual who only knows one culture and is confined to behaving as that one culture tends to dictate! The intercultural experience and the learned empathy is one of the most important advantages that study abroad offers.

ENGLISH PROFICIENCY

An individual's mastery and proficiency in both speaking and writing in English will be a key factor as to how successful an individual will be in the US because he/she will have to be able to communicate clearly and logically in the English language. Having high test scores on the TOEFL or IELTS will not mean anything if one cannot communicate effectively in English with other Americans and international students. Although Americans are known to be friendly and outgoing, some Americans may not be as understanding and patient as many Asians might be towards any white, Caucasian American in a place like Tokyo where the American might be struggling to communicate in the Japanese language with the local people.

The majority of US university students will lack "language empathy" towards foreign students. This stems from the fact that in the US, only about 1% of university students go on study abroad programs, so most US students will not have any idea of the language and cultural challenges and hardships that foreign students experience when they first come to the US. Moreover, the majority of Americans only speak one language–English. And so they have never experienced learning in a second or third language where one may not be able to understand what is going on in class.

For those Americans who do go on study abroad programs, many tend to participate in more insulated types of study abroad programs which usually tend to be short-term for four-weeks or sometimes a semester. Many of these short-term programs are also group-oriented programs that include other US students and are often led by an American faculty person. This type of study abroad experience would tend to be relatively insulated and safe. In addition, many of these types of short-term and semester programs are primarily for language study. The students are studying the country's language, they are **not** studying course subjects in a foreign language. There is a huge difference here. It would be similar to international students coming to the US and studying only in the English language programs (ESL), not in the regular academic content program. And although with most US short-term programs, they offer many opportunities for the American students to interact with host country students and host families, the tendency would still be an overall sheltered study abroad experience as most of the language and culture classes will be with primarily US students. Moreover, the subject-based courses that the Americans take in addition to language courses will be taught in English, not the native language of the country.

Even in the rare cases when some American students pursue a degree from a foreign country outside of the US, it is almost always at an English-speaking country like the UK or Australia. And although the UK and Australia are technically "foreign countries," both are western countries where English is the spoken language and their cultural values and social behaviors are quite similar to the US.

Although these American students have a study abroad experience, it is not to the same degree nor with the same depth and inherent struggles that most foreign students will undertake when studying in a second or third language in the US. Half the battle to graduation for many foreign students is to successfully pass regular academic courses in English, and not their mother tongue.

It is extremely challenging when an individual has to pursue a full degree program in a second language, compounded with having to do so in a country where major adjustments to the nuances of the culture and customs are required. I would guess that out of the 1% of US students who do go on study abroad programs, perhaps only about 1% of the 1% actually do participate in a degree program in another language and country, unless they are recent immigrants to the US who are already bilingual in English and possibly another language, for example, Spanish.

These types of students could pursue a degree program in another language because they are already proficient in a second language. However, outside of these types of bilingual students, most American students would not attempt to do a degree program in another country in a second language other than English.

My point here is that due to the above reasons, it will be very difficult for US students to understand or empathize with the language and culture difficulties and struggles that non-western foreign students experience in the US. It reflects back to the Cherokee Indians' proverb that you cannot really understand what someone is going through until you have walked in their shoes. Therefore, foreign students should not expect US students and friends to understand their language/culture "wall" because US students have never experienced what foreign students experience daily while studying abroad.

For foreign students, as they attempt to speak casually with American friends, it is not only about speaking English correctly, but there is a certain rhythm and speed to a conversation or verbal exchange among friends. Conversations are like playing "catch ball" whereby there is usually a tempo of quickly going back and forth in the conversation among those engaged in the exchange. As a result, one's speaking response time and speed is many times more important than necessarily being able to use grammatically correct sentences when speaking informally with American friends. If a person is too slow in speaking or responding, some Americans may not wait for the person to complete his/her sentences or thoughts.

That is why before going to the US, it is very important to work on improving one's proficiency in English oral communications skills. From the moment you arrive on campus, it will make a tremendous difference in the quality and experiences of studying abroad. One might also want to specifically work on developing a smooth rhythm and speed so that a conversation in English becomes more natural and not appear to be forced.

One will find that being able to quickly respond to someone may be the key to communicating well in the US. Whether it is attending an English language school or doing a language exchange with a native English speaker in the home country prior to your departure to the US, you will need to start this spoken language training as early as possible. I would say that it might be recommended to begin at least one to two years in advance. By doing so, it will make one's life much easier and less stressful after arriving in the US.

It is also important to be able to communicate effectively when writing in English. It is essential to know the usual sequence of nouns, verbs, adverbs, and adjectives when writing in English. There are some basic rules that govern paragraph and sentence construction that an individual can quickly master with proper training. Depending on the written communication patterns of one's native language, the English language has its own idiosyncrasies that need to be mastered. For example, in many non-English languages, the verb is usually written before the noun is identified, whereas in English, the noun usually precedes the verb that describes the action of the noun.

Even if one has a high TOEFL or IELTS score, that does not equate to being able to write well in English. In any language, academic writing more than speaking can be the most difficult thing to master. I have read many students' essays written in English and although they could speak English well, their written English bordered on being unintelligible. And to try and help them rewrite their essay would have taken them so much more time than just trying to write the entire essay over again.

So, while a lot of emphasis has been placed on being able to speak in English effectively while studying abroad, one should not disregard the importance of also being able to master English writing skills. While it might be secondary to being able to speak English well, it should not be disregarded because good English writing skills will be required as part of everyday life and especially in one's college course work and eventually in one's job and career.

As you prepare for studying abroad, one of the best ways to learn how to write better is to read as much as you can in English. Read a newspaper, magazines, books, etc., even the internet is a good source, but you must read real articles and well written texts. Just reading Facebook or Line entries in English will not really help you except to learn more American slangs and shortcuts to American expressions. If you want to increase your vocabulary, learn better sentence structure for when you write, and get better grades–read, read, and read in English!

Upon arrival, if you are still not confident in your English writing ability, but have qualified to take regular subject based courses, some of you may still want to take one English as a Second Language (ESL) writing course to improve your writing. The course and credit probably won't count towards your graduation requirements, but a good writing teacher can help change your academic life. Of course, it potentially will cost more because it will take you longer to graduate as most of the ESL credits cannot be used for graduation. But if you invest in getting a solid English language base and strong study skills, it could really change your ability and attitude once you start taking regular courses.

Also, I would suggest to all students to visit the writing and learning centers on their US campuses. All US campuses have some form of a learning or writing center where tutors can help you with subject study and writing. I advise students to start going to the learning center from the very first week they start school in the US. Go and meet the learning/writing center staff and start to get help long before you actually need help.

Some universities will let you take a "hybrid" type of class schedule where you can take maybe two ESL courses and then 2-3 easier regular subject courses to help you gradually assimilate into the real world of academic life in English. But again, the courses you take in ESL may not be counted towards your graduation. However, I do believe if you can invest early in improving your English language skills, it will pay you back ten folds later on down the line. Those who have bad habits and do not receive training or help to fix their English language problems will often always repeat the same mistakes which eventually will become "fossilized," meaning that they can no longer correct themselves and they will forever be making the same mistakes.

PRESENTATION SKILLS

Many foreign students are usually not as skillful at making presentations or doing public speaking in front of people in comparison to Americans or those from western cultures. This difference has no connection to a person's intelligence level or ability. It has to do with the lack of experience and training and practice in their K-12 education and even throughout their university education. When I was teaching in Japan, I asked my university freshmen students every year, how many of them had previously done presentations or public speaking in front of their classmates or other people. Only about 5% said they had done some kind of presentation in high school. The rest had never previously done any type of public presentation.

Since 95% of my students had said they had not done any type of presentation before, I would teach them the basics and get them to practice and do presentations which required organizing their thoughts, making a Power Point presentation, speaking in front of the class, and teaching them to speak without reading their presentation notes.

When I taught presentation skills to my university students in Japan, the six basic public speaking rules I used were:

1) Make eye contact with the entire room of listeners
2) Use natural hand movements and gestures and some speakers will even move and walk around during a presentation
3) Ensure the volume of your voice is loud enough so you can be heard in the back of the classroom
4) Do NOT read your presentation except to possibly summarize or emphasize what might be on your Power Point slide
5) Speak with confidence and about something you know very well
6) Smile and attempt to establish a personal connection with the audience

Unfortunately, classes related to public speaking, speech or debate, are usually not taught or offered in Japan or other Asian countries during the K-12 grades and even at the university level. In contrast in the US, when my nephew, Jace, was five years old and in kindergarten, the kindergarten classes all did something weekly called "Show and Tell." Each student would take a turn in front of the class and talk about what they did during the past weekend. Thus, for Americans, their first presentation is in kindergarten and there are speech assignments and other public speaking activities throughout their K-12 schooling.

Therefore, it is only natural that Americans would be more comfortable and skilled in doing presentations and public speaking. Studying in the US will initially be very stressful for most foreign students when they have to give their first presentations before their classmates in English. Nevertheless, it is the best place to learn because Americans are, by most accounts, some of the best presenters in the world. This is a great opportunity where foreign students can learn from Americans who are skilled at presentations, primarily by observing and adopting good presentation techniques and style. I believe that good presentation and oratory skills are some of the most important skills necessary for all students' future careers and life in general.

Although Americans are relatively good at making presentations, it doesn't mean they don't have anxieties about speaking in front of a group. But they have been raised in an education system that teaches students to be able to speak in public. Throughout the world, the three universally worst fears people often have are fear of heights, fear of flying, and the fear of having to speak in public. Thus, it is only natural that presentations and public speaking will be very stressful to most individuals, especially if the person lacks the experience.

In American university classes, many upper level courses have doing presentations as part of the requirement to pass the class and get a good grade. So the two major challenges for foreign students will be doing their presentations in front of their classmates and teacher, and of course, doing it in English. Needless to say, oftentimes, due to unfamiliarity with the language and inexperience, the foreign student will have to work and practice at least twice or three times as hard as their American classmates to make a good presentation.

PRESENTATION SKILLS

It stands to reason that the more experience and practice a foreign student can get speaking in front of people before leaving their home country, the easier time he/she will have after arriving in the US. But usually there are still big differences between a typical class presentation in the foreign student's home country and a presentation in the US. I think the quality and skill of classroom lectures and presentations conducted by foreign university faculty and US faculty, can reflect the big difference and general ability of presentation skills and public speaking in each country.

In many foreign universities, in many of the classes, the professor or instructor will sit in the front of the class and lecture, sometimes using the blackboard but rarely using Power Point presentations or video or multi-media options. In foreign countries, it is usually standard operating procedure to use a chalkboard or whiteboard and at other times to sit at a podium or table and lecture by reading from one's lecture notes.

In the US, most of the time the professor or instructor will be standing and may be moving around in the front of the class while lecturing. Most use Power Point or some kind of media presentation mode. Many may use a variety of video and other multi-media in a single presentation. In the US, many of the university lectures and K-12 teacher lessons have almost an entertainment-like quality to them. And this is where one can visibly see and compare the distinct differences of presentation styles between the US and foreign universities.

One of the keys to a well-received presentation is for the speaker to display confidence. Confidence can often be demonstrated by the speaker's mastery of the presentation content. If one is not comfortable or feels like he/she doesn't know the content well, there is a good chance that it will also be noticed by the audience. Consequently, one must really know the content well.

PRESENTATION SKILLS

Watch and learn from really good presenters on the Ted Talks on You Tube. Many of the presenters have charisma and energy where they can hold the audience captive, but they also have to know the subject of their presentation very well. And the best US speakers do not memorize anything, they can speak naturally and extemporaneously.

Compare that with a poor presentation where it appears that the presenter is simply regurgitating words and does not really know the content being presented. Subsequently, if you must make a presentation on a topic that you may be a bit uncomfortable delivering, you really have to put in an extra effort to truly understand the subject matter so that you can deliver your presentation with relative comfort.

The first step to achieving confidence is to practice, practice, and do more practice going over the presentation. This does not mean to memorize your presentation or speech like what is many times expected in some non-western education systems, but you need to organize your thoughts in some sort of sequence so that you can emphasize the critical points you intend to make. This can best be achieved if you know the content material very well. The more times one practices the presentation, the greater the likelihood that one will be become more comfortable and natural with the content.

If the content is too complicated and a bit above the audience's knowledge of the topic, chances are that the presentation will be considered confusing or difficult to comprehend. However, if the content is below the audience's level of understanding of the subject matter, the presentation most likely will be considered boring and a waste of time. People want to learn something new from a presentation, even if it is just a bit here and a bit there and it is at a level that they can relate to intellectually. The goal of any presentation is to get the audience to think about the presented subject matter. When a speaker can achieve this, the presentation should be considered a success.

There are many other things one can do to practice to become a good speaker, but what has been previously mentioned are the six basic rules that are the most essential to a good presentation. If you watch a US leader like former President Obama or even now President Donald Trump give a speech, they will usually have a kind of eloquence or charisma when they speak. The way they talk, the way they use their hand movements, the way they pause at the right time, the way they repeat certain points, the way they look out at the audience–all make for a good presentation.

In turn, a good presentation is like a great performance. Therefore, if one thinks of a presentation as a form of a performance, it may put the activity in a totally different light and how one approaches a presentation in the future. With this mindset, it may give new meaning to what it might take to give a good performance and get people to think about your presentation subject.

Many foreign leaders and teachers are not as dynamic as their American counterparts. They usually look down reading their presentation notes while they speak. The tone of their voice is usually more monotone. And perhaps this is acceptable in some countries, but in the US, this style of speech would be considered boring and a very low level of public speaking. Most people would stop listening after a while. For many Americans, if the material and content are not presented well, it is very difficult to keep listening to the presentation and people will eventually tune you out.

In many Asian countries, the emphasis is put on the content and information and not so much effort is put into the actual presentation and delivery. In the past, that may have been acceptable, but in today's millennial world where young people seem to have much shorter attention spans, a speaker has to be able to package and deliver the presentation in a much more exciting or at least interesting way or the intended audience will stop listening.

English is usually the language used in international arenas, so naturally Americans leaders have the advantage to present well, especially when compared to watching a foreign leader trying to speak in English or having his speech translated. If you watched on You Tube the press conference of when Prime Minister Abe met President Donald Trump for the first time on February 10, 2017 in the US, his opening speech was quite puzzling about what he was talking about. After the speech, and during the question and answer session, even if Prime Minister Abe can understand some English and had the questions translated for him, there were misses that made him look awkward (https://www.youtube.com/watch?v=a9bDERrKYWI).

Prime Minister Abe opened his speech, which was translated into English, with a reference to his name being "A-be," but some Americans might read it as "Abe" (as in Abe Lincoln), and he went on to try and connect his name and Abe Lincoln (without ever saying President Abe Lincoln's name) and how the Japanese were so impressed by the US 150 years ago as the champion of democracy while Japan was under the rule of the shogunate. It sounded very random and made little sense.

And without any background knowledge of where Japan and the US were 150 years ago, one cannot even guess what he was talking about. I am sure Prime Minister Abe had a Japanese speechwriter who probably graduated from Tokyo University that wrote that speech and it may have been appropriate in Japan for a Japanese audience, but in English, Americans could not follow or understand the point that Abe was trying to make. In short, the overall impression of Americans who were listening was "What did he just say???"

After the speech, during the question and answer period, the first question a reporter asked was to President Trump about the use of executive power and if he would sign a new travel ban. The second question was to Prime Minster Abe about America's withdrawal of the Trans-Pacific Partnership (TPP) and how that affects US influence in the region and if there are any possible new trade deals with the US.

After President Trump spoke about the security of the country, the court process and keeping America safe, Prime Minister Abe seemed a bit caught off guard and then talked about refugees and terrorism in the world and that both countries would have to work together on global issues with the international community. Then he added that immigration control and policy are technically domestic issues, so he would refrain from making any comments. He never answered the question to him about TPP and he talked about something that was not even asked of President Trump. It made Japan and Prime Minister Abe look irrelevant and somewhat out of place in that setting.

That is why English comprehension and fluency, as well as how to give effective presentations and speak in front of others is so important. I believe that the way people do presentations and speak in public is a reflection of the respective education systems, methods of teaching and learning, and what is considered important to the respective countries.

For many, such as in Asia, education tends to put a strong emphasis on the written test. Asian teachers are usually not rewarded or recognized for teaching in a more innovative and dynamic way. No one encourages them to teach in a more interactive way. There are usually no awards or recognition for a teacher or instructor who teaches in an inspiring and riveting way.

In most cases, the goal in Asia is for teachers to get their students to pass the tests and exams so that the students can get into a good university and then get a good job. That should not, however, be an excuse as to why Asian students may be at a disadvantage in making presentations. It just means that most Asian students have to work harder on their "performances."

The US is much more focused and experienced in active and experiential teaching. If foreign students could experience this type of active teaching and learning, I believe it would open up a whole new creative world for them and enhance their ability to truly reach their full potential. Then those who eventually become teachers would have a profound influence on the future of teaching and education in their country into the 21st century.

SOCIAL SKILLS

Social skills can be defined as one exhibiting acceptable manners, having effective communication skills as situations dictate, being able to read a situation, demonstrating appropriate social etiquette and protocol, having good timing, taking turns to talk, and having the ability to relate and behave in a socially accepted way with other people. The skills include both verbal and non-verbal communication.

Thus, generally, someone who has good social skills will be able to more easily connect with people and make friends. On the other hand, someone who lacks social skills may turn people off or offend them without even realizing that they have done so. For example, in Japan, they have the expression describing these types of people as "KY" or "Kuuki o yomenai," which basically translates to "someone who cannot read the air," or someone who lacks social skills. These people struggle to make friends and find their place in society.

What constitutes good social skills and acceptable social behavior can vary from country to country. In the US, good social skills involve such things as being friendly and outgoing, making eye contact, smiling, having a firm or assertive handshake, being comfortable in engaging in "small talk" as situations dictate, appearing to be approachable, etc.

If you have ever been to an international conference with attendees from different countries, you can definitely see the differences in social skills of different countries when attendees meet one another for the first time. From what I have observed after attending many international education conferences, many times the foreign attendees feel somewhat awkward or the timing is just a bit off when they are meeting someone for the first time. Part of it can be attributed to some foreign attendees not being as proficient in English, but the other half of the problem is usually their inability to make conversation and establish a connection with people from other countries. The situation of meeting someone for the first time leads us into another important social skill area called "small talk."

SMALL TALK

"Small talk" is generally what is said to start off a conversation with someone whom you are meeting for the first time. "Small talk" is usually the "ice breaker" that starts the conversation between two or more people. Americans tend to be very good at this aspect of social skills when first meeting other people. There may be a variety of reasons why Americans tend to be very natural at "small talk," but first, when Americans meet non-Americans, the language used is almost always English. This tends to provide an American with a definite advantage to engage in "small talk."

Secondly, the American character tends to be quite outgoing and friendly, in contrast with some cultures in Asia, which tend to initially emphasize being more reserved and respectful of status or position. Americans are usually not afraid of smiling, extending their arm to shake hands, and taking the initiative of introducing themselves.

This is where many foreign faculty and students may struggle. For example, in Asian societies, usually a mutual acquaintance will make the appropriate introductions. It is not a common practice in most Asian countries to just walk up to someone one doesn't know, introduce him/herself, and start a conversation. There is also the issue of seniority, perceived rank, or age whereby a more respected leader with established seniority, rank, or age will tend not to take the initiative or initiate an introduction with someone of lower status or rank. Usually subordinates will introduce the new guests to their leader or boss or superior.

Taking the situation one step further, for example, imagine you are attending an international conference that has 5,000 people in attendance and you do not know a single person attending the event. Furthermore, you arrive late and the welcome reception has already started and it looks like almost everyone is already talking to someone. You feel very alone. What should you do? Return to your hotel room? Grab a drink and stand in the corner like a "wall flower?" Look for other attendees from your country and talk to them in your native language?

Or you could take the risk and assertively extend your arm for a handshake, introduce yourself, and ask an opening question. No one faced with this kind of predicament, including most Americans, particularly enjoy this type of situation. But most Americans will often not hesitate to approach someone they don't know and introduce themselves to start a conversation.

For a Japanese person, it might be as simple as saying "Hi, my name is Ichiro and I'm from Japan. Where are you from?" This potentially sets the stage for more "small talk" about the person's position, whether the individual has attended previous conferences, if the person knows anyone else at the conference, etc. Since most people are most interested in talking about themselves, starting with a genuine interest in getting to know others is a good starting point. As long as one stays away from controversial issues or "hot button" topics like religion, politics, etc., the focus of "small talk" conversations is usually very cordial. By continuing to mingle and engaging in more "small talk" with other attendees, one can create more of a friendly feel for the event.

The key to "small talk" is the willingness to take the initiative to engage another individual and begin the conversation. Without taking the initiative, an individual is reliant on others to take the initiative to begin a conversation. Since, as has been stated earlier, most people would normally be uncomfortable in these kinds of situations, there may be very few "small talk" initiators at these kinds of events so by taking the initiative, one can really benefit and will probably be noticed by others as someone who is very outgoing and friendly. You are leaving people with a good first impression of yourself and that is the start of all relationships and business deals.

To be good at "small talk" is a very important skill to have, especially as a study abroad student. For a variety of reasons many foreign students struggle with "small talk." For example, in Japan there is an aging cultural norm that "silence is golden" or that you generally only speak when one is spoken to. As a result, most Japanese don't usually strike up conversations with people they don't know, unlike Americans and westerners who tend to do so.

Take for example at the supermarket in the US where many customers are standing and waiting in line for their turn to check out and pay for items. Americans might tend to be more likely to start up a conversation with others in the line or the cashier who is ringing up the food and collecting the money. This is an example of "small talk" at its best. To do so appropriately requires one to read the situation as to the other person's receptivity to engaging in "small talk."

Not everyone in the US is necessarily open to engaging in "small talk," but in these types of situations, one can generally find that a friendly smile can work wonders to establish first contact. Casually talking with the cashier over the weather or the price of items is very common for customers waiting in line to pay. The conversation is usually very light, upbeat and many times humorous.

I have never seen this type of "small talk" behavior and interaction at any supermarket in Asia. In Asia, the cashier's job is to ring up the items and collect the money, not to make casual conversation with customers. If they behaved in a similar fashion as their American counterparts, Asian customers would think that the cashiers were not taking their jobs seriously.

The possible reason why "small talk" can be difficult for many Asian students is that attempting to make "small talk" with anyone who is a stranger requires taking a risk. The risk is that when you say something to someone or simply introduce yourself, the other party may not understand your English or accent. They may ignore you or make you feel awkward or uncomfortable. For whatever the reason, you may be misunderstood or viewed as someone strange and it may be very embarrassing, a "loss of face."

Thus, to some people, trying to make "small talk" might be stressful and considered a risk. But you should never stop taking the risk in appropriate situations for that is the only way you will learn how to improve your "small talk" skills. Moreover, you would be surprised how sometimes those "small talk" conversations at a conference or event may lead to becoming "big talk" discussions like a possible job offer, making a sale, or making a new friend. That is why practicing and learning to be skilled and natural at "small talk" is extremely important in the US.

An entire book could be written on just "small talk" skills and maybe that may be my next book! But to offer potential study abroad students some general suggestions, the first and foremost is that the better your English proficiency, the easier it will be to engage in "small talk." Secondly, be observant and aware of the situation you are in. Always look and watch what people are doing, what they are talking about, what they are wearing, and their gestures and movements.

"Small talk" is most effective when it is related and appropriate to a specific situation. Just talking about anything not relevant to a situation is not very effective as it could be interpreted that you just like to talk for talking's sake, even when there is no apparent reason to do so. By being able to read the situation, you can decide how to start, how to keep a conversation going or politely ending a "small talk" conversation.

It also helps to pay special attention to the other person's eyes and where they are looking during the conversation and to seek confirmation through their body language that they are interested in what is being said. Always try to be observant and aware. Lastly, take the risk to start a conversation with "small talk." As they say in America, "No guts, no glory!"

COMPLIMENTING OTHERS

In the US, among friends and peers, there is a lot of joking and teasing that goes on, but there is also a lot of complimenting that happens. In fact, complimenting is one of the best ways to begin "small talk". Many

COMPLIMENTING OTHERS

Americans will begin a conversation with a compliment. "Wow, that is a cool t-shirt!" or "I really like the color of your scarf" or "That's an awesome pendant you are wearing." Now the main point is that an individual has to be sincere and genuine with any remarks. An individual should not make up anything or just flatter someone for the sake of making "small talk." These types of situations above, however, do not apply when individuals are deliberately making these remarks to tease each other. Therefore, good judgment and discretion is necessary when complimenting another person.

Furthermore, an individual doesn't want to be known as a "brown-noser" or the person who over compliments insincerely. So do a quick assessment of a person and look for something that one can sincerely and genuinely compliment him/her on or something that positively stands out about the person. And if one doesn't find anything to compliment about, then talk about something else such as the weather or the price of university books.

I have asked many Asian students from the different Asian countries, "Do your parents ever compliment you?" About 90% of the time, the answer is no. If they say yes, then I ask them what did they say to you? One student said that her mom sometimes says, "Thank you." I would not call this a compliment, but more as an expression of appreciation. Other students said things like my dad said that I studied hard. But the compliments are usually far and fewer in an Asian culture.

In Asian cultures, complimenting one's family and close friends in their presence is not very common. There is also a sense of being embarrassed to compliment someone because many times words of endearment and praise are not very common or frequently expressed in Asian cultures. Asian cultural values tend to put oneself or one's family down while stressing the qualities or accomplishments of the other person or family.

I believe that this is more of a sign of respect and cultural norm than serious complimenting. The bigger the gap between my humbleness and your "greatness," is a sign of respect to the other person. In short, in some Asian cultures, the bigger the status gap between individuals, the greater the respect that is being shown.

When I visit Asian university and high school classrooms, I sometimes do an exercise about complimenting. I compliment one of the students who is sitting in front of me. I may say something like, "Wow, that is a nice sweater you are wearing!" And he/she will usually laugh or smile and not know how to respond. I then usually explain that the easiest response for an American is "Thank you!" and smile. But I also add that in Japan, when you compliment people, many of them would do the "windshield wiper" movement with their hands going back and forth saying, "No, no, no!" and then they sometimes add that they got the clothing item on sale or that it is old, or say something to show a degree of modesty.

In much of Japan and Asia, there is still this tendency to put oneself down because being humble is a virtue in Asia. I can still see this behavior in Hawaii among the older Asian Americans to be modest and humble because these are virtues from an Asian point of view. But in the US, a simple "Thank you" and a smile is probably the best if a person is not sure of what other response would be appropriate. This is where the values of east and west differ greatly.

I then continue my complimenting exercise in class. I ask a student to compliment another student. I say be sincere and compliment her/him. At first they are caught off guard but they usually are able to quickly look at the person and say something like, "That is a nice handbag." The other student will usually answer with what I just told them as the best answer and respond by smiling and saying "Thank you." Then I would ask that person how did the compliment make her feel? And she would reply,

"Happy." I would then ask the student giving the compliment how did it make him/her feel that their classmate felt happy about the compliment he/she gave her? The answer would usually be "Happy" or "Good."

So, I would then turn to the class and say, "He/she is happy that she liked the compliment. She is happy that she was complimented. Both people are then happy. Did it cost any money?" The students shake their heads and say "No." I then say, "So why don't we compliment one another more? It is a "win-win" situation and doesn't cost any money!" And in the US, complimenting is very common. And if individuals are very skilled and sincere with compliments to other people, they will potentially be able to make many friends and start conversations wherever they may go.

In the eyes of many Asian parents, American parents may look like they over compliment and exaggerate the actual accomplishments of their children. Some might say that over complimenting is giving the child a false sense of believing that he/she is doing something well when in actuality, it is very minimal. This misplaced emphasis could lead to the child being very disappointed when he/she someday realizes the truth.

Sometimes this is true, but according to some psychologists, sincere complimenting can be very good for the child's self-esteem and confidence. I think the main point here is to be honest and sincere about the compliments that a parent gives their children and friends. Right or wrong, that is how most younger Americans have been brought up and where they are today. This needs to be taken into consideration when engaging with younger people in the US.

In Asia, due to the culture being more reserved, modest and humble, people are less likely to compliment one another. Many Asian parents often raise their children with very few compliments and tend to push them to continually do better the next time. It is a totally different child rearing system when comparing it to the US. Asian parents want to keep their child humble and not get "big headed," and they want them to continue working and studying hard, to improve, and always do better.

In the American culture, the way of raising children is quite different. Many parents are very quick to positively compliment and reinforce when their child is doing something good, even if it is only a minor thing. They are frequently saying, "Way to go!" with a fist bump, or "Great job!" or "That was amazing!"

This is all a reflection of the childrearing "self-esteem movement" that started in America about forty years ago. People who felt that their parents were too strict in placing controls on their lives or whom did not want to discipline their own children because they saw their parenting role as being a "friend" to their children, rather than being a "parent," began a movement to make the American child believe that he/she was a unique and special individual.

Under the "self-esteem movement," children were made to feel important even if they had no unique attribute; they may have had greater freedom to do things their own way; and they were often recognized for insignificant accomplishments. The basis was to build the child's self-esteem on the belief that a child who felt good about his/herself would grow into a more optimistic, productive, and responsible adult. Unfortunately, in some instances, children of this generation have a somewhat unrealistic perception of their abilities and/or who they really are or how others perceive them.

A good example of this is what happened to Little League baseball programs. When I played Little League baseball, only the championship team received a trophy and the focus was on the collective team effort. Today, most Little League players all receive a trophy, regardless of whether the team won the championship or not. As a result, younger Americans today may be more prone to think more highly of themselves than others who grew up in an earlier time or are from another culture.

HOW TO BECOME A GOOD CONVERSATIONALIST

You can be popular and have many friends in the US or anywhere in the world if you are a good conversationalist. It could be a person's most valuable skill that will be an essential part of a successful life, a productive work career, and potentially a larger network of real friends. More importantly, if one becomes a good conversationalist, it can potentially help an individual find and keep a boyfriend/girlfriend or husband/wife. The most important thing for a successful, long lasting marriage or relationship is not about having a lot of money, fame or only good looks. It is often more about finding someone that one can easily and comfortably talk and communicate with for the rest of one's life. However, for this to mutually work, both partners will need to be an active listener and good communicator.

Know a little about everything

To be a good conversationalist, one ideally has to be quite knowledgeable about a broad range of topics so he/she can talk with anyone whom one meets at any given time or place. It really helps to know something about a variety of things. And this includes everything from world events, the current news, TV, popular culture, local sports, the local news and the area one lives in, and whatever else might be important to the people one will happen to meet and talk with. Of course, one cannot expect to be an expert on everything, but one should know at least something about most general subjects.

When I travel to different countries for university visits, the first thing I do when I arrive and check in to the hotel is to turn on the television and look for the local news in English, if it is available. I also buy a local English language newspaper and skim through it. I pick up news tidbits and stories on what is going on locally, maybe a teacher's strike or a mining accident. Then when I meet local people from the hotel, at the restaurants, or at the universities, I may tactfully bring up the news topics I have read about to engage someone in a conversation.

Usually the local people are very surprised that I know about what was going on locally and they almost always would actively talk about local issues and news. People like to talk about what they know and are familiar with. It also enriches me to know more about the area and people, as well as it is more knowledge and information to know for potentially the next local person I talk to whom I may be able to ask questions at an even deeper level with the new information from the last person.

So, it ends up being a "win-win." The people I meet who are from that country may be impressed or flattered that I was up to date and astute to knowing about what was going on locally. It is also a great way for a foreigner to learn more about the local people and area and it allows an individual to engage in more meaningful conversations rather than just "small talk."

Asking questions

To be a good conversationalist is to naturally be curious about everything. Ask questions about things that one may be curious and want to know more about. If someone is curious about everything, asking questions becomes very natural and the person should be able to start conversations very easily. Asking questions also tends to show that the person is interested in the topic, the area and the people, and helps to establish a rapport with whomever one is engaging with in a conversation. And that is a high compliment for anyone and will really help an individual make friends, business acquaintances, and contribute to a much more exciting and well-informed life.

HOW TO BECOME A GOOD CONVERSATIONALIST

Always remember that most people in a comfortable situation enjoy talking about their lives. The ability to get people to open up about themselves and share with others is a great skill to have. Everyone has a story to tell and if a person is a good conversationalist, one can usually get others to open up and share more about themselves. Some people refer to this ability as "disarming" or having someone let down their emotional guard.

There are different personal qualities to being a good conversationalist. Some people are funny or witty and others are knowledgeable and expressive. Still others can be very engaging and they can inspire and encourage or motivate people through their conversations. Everyone has different strengths and every individual should first know their conversational strengths and try to utilize the strengths that they possess.

I cannot emphasize enough that if a person is a good conversationalist, it will help him/her in every aspect of their present and future life. Being a good conversationalist is both an art, as well as a skill. In the event that an individual is not very good at conversation, keep practicing and be very observant of other good conversationalists. Try to watch and listen to what makes someone a good conversationalist such as what questions do they ask, how do they take turns speaking, how do they ask follow up questions, their body language, etc. This will help one become better at being more interesting and engaging with people.

Here the key may be in the concept of "disarming" or getting someone to comfortably let their guard down. A good conversationalist in any language or culture, will attempt to have the other person "disarm" in the course of the conversation in order to bring down people's defenses and have them open up more honestly. However, in order to do this, one must also be willing to "disarm" and be open because a genuine, meaningful, and productive conversation cannot occur while only one person "disarms" while the other party to the conversation continues to be "on guard." Conversations such as this with one party "armed" and the other "disarmed" are generally one-sided and unproductive and do not fit the definition of a good conversation.

That is why being a good conversationalist has very important carryover benefits. Long-term relationships are based on each individual being willing to "disarm" in the process of a conversation. It is this sense of intimacy that bonds people together. Without it, many times relationships are shattered because one party may be holding back important information that the other party may need to hear to have a better understanding of a situation.

Study abroad in the US is a good way to test and hone your conversational and English skills. This is because first of all, it is a challenge to be able to be a good conversationalist in the English language when speaking with Americans. Most Americans are talkers. They like to talk and discuss things. A foreigner must be quite proficient with his/her English skills to participate and reach the level of being a good conversationalist in the US.

This is one area where the more chances an individual has to practice and improve one's skills, the better the person will become and one's comfort level should also increase over time. Setting a personal goal to be a good conversationalist while one is on a study abroad program is highly recommended. For example, in the one to four years of studying abroad in the US, work on trying to become the best conversationalist in your dormitory or your class or among your friends.

When having a conversation, there should also be a certain conversational rhythm like when two people are playing "catch ball." One should be sensitive not to dominate the conversation. Actually, a smart conversationalist will initially do a lot of the listening of the other party. By doing so, an individual can take in and think over the information being shared before responding. Trying to respond without enough information doesn't always work because a lot more assumptions may have to be made about what the other person is actually saying.

Consistent with the concept of "disarming," the more people can talk and share about themselves, the greater the chance that they will end up liking the other party because he/she listened and showed a sincere interest in them. Everyone wants to feel important and significant. By actively and intently listening to someone, a person can nonverbally let the other party know that he/she is significant.

Sometimes an individual will meet someone who will dominate the conversation too much and the person being talked to is just listening without any chance to be a part of the conversation. If this happens and one wants to leave the conversation, just be tactful and tell the other person that one has another commitment to attend to and politely excuse oneself from the exchange. To be overly patient often leads to frustration over the lack of assertiveness to get out of the situation, in addition to wasting precious time. At other times when people are talking about their passion, they may excitingly dominate the conversation without even knowing the affect it is having on the other person.

But if the seemingly one-way conversation is inspiring and interesting, it might be entertaining and beneficial to let the individual go on and just absorb what they are saying. So there is no rule set in stone as to how to best deal with every situation. Every situation needs to be approached on a case-by-case, person-by-person experience. But the goal is to be able to speak and talk with as many people as one can on a variety of topics that may come up.

Remembering names

Dale Carnegie was the legend of American public speaking and was the pioneer author who wrote about public speaking and social skills back in 1936. His book has been translated into numerous languages and he has sold over 30 million copies throughout the world. In his book, "How to Win Friends and Influence People," he wrote that the sweetest and most important word to any person is their name. And I have learned through the years how true this is. If a person correctly remembers someone's name and can use it in the conversation, it adds a different level of familiarity and connection.

Some people, like myself, have a difficult time remembering names, especially if the names are associated with individuals from a non-western country. When I meet someone for the first time, I try to use their name tactfully over and over during the conversation.

A conversation may go something like this when meeting someone for the first time in California:

Me: Hi, I am Mike Matsuno from Hawaii.

Ryan: Nice to meet you, I am Ryan Sputnik.

Me: Are you from California, **Ryan**?

Ryan: No, I moved to California five years ago.

Me: How do you like it?

Ryan: The weather is unbeatable but there are a lot of people. I am from a small town in the Midwest.

Me: So **Ryan**, what do you miss about your small town?

And the conversation continues…

Anyway, in the previous example, I would try to use Ryan's name repeatedly throughout the conversation, so the more I said it, the more chances it had of going into my long-term memory file. And people feel closer to a person when he/she uses their name. Saying the person's name throughout the conversation is a good habit to have as it eventually should become very natural for a person who practices this technique.

I even use this technique with people whom I don't know and who are wearing company name tags like at McDonald's or Starbucks. I will quickly look at the individual's name on their name tag (i.e. John) before ordering and say something like, "Let's see, John. What do you think would be good today?" Or when thanking them at the end, I might say something like "Thank you, John. Hope you have a great day!" I believe that someone who is just serving people all day is touched and happy when you identify them by their name.

When I worked at McDonald's when I was in college, I will never forget the person who inspired me about the power of using my name. Her name was Jennifer and she worked at the local travel agency. She would come in from time to time and she always had a beautiful smile and used my name, "Hi Mike, so what's good today?" or "Hi Mike, how are the Big Macs selling today?" I was always very touched and over 30 years later, I still remember Jennifer, how she looked, her voice, and mannerisms. So why not acknowledge and use someone's name if it makes him/her happy, may improve your service, leaves a good impression, and doesn't cost anything? It's a "win-win" situation.

I also suggest if one meets someone on campus or somewhere and there is a good chance to meet him/her again or perhaps an individual wants to meet them again, I would strongly suggest remembering something about that individual besides their name. Some piece of information that one learned during the first meeting with him/her. Maybe he/she plays hockey or has been to China or something that the next time when one meets the person, one can skillfully work the information into the conversation. It will also help to leave a good impression that one remembered something about them in addition to their name.

People like to be recognized. They feel significant and "special" when someone takes the time and effort to make them feel noticed and appreciated. If for example, I met Ryan the first time and he said that he played hockey. The next time if I happened to meet Ryan again, after saying "Hi, Ryan, good to see you again", I might say something like, "I remembered you said you moved to California from the Midwest. Have you had much chance to play hockey here?" I am quite sure that Ryan would be happy to talk about hockey and very impressed that I remembered that he moved from the Midwest and played hockey. This is a good way to build a relationship, leave a good impression and make a possible friend.

Small talk and remembering names are very important for the first and second meetings, but the long-term goal is to become a good conversationalist. If an individual is able to become a good conversationalist and good listener, that person will most likely have many friends, his/her personal network will increase, and the prospects of being successful in life are greatly increased. As the data shows, there is a direct correlation to having good personal relationships and being happy.

Always remember that everyone wants to talk and has something to say, even if at first they may seem shy or reserved. If a person is skillful in their "small talk" abilities and conversational skills, eventually the individual should be able to get the other person to open up and share more things about themselves. Insightful questions that pertain to them and related topics that they probably would want to talk about are the key points.

People usually love to talk about their high school life, their most memorable vacation, their interests and passion, and so on. Also as an individual becomes more skilled in conversation, the person will be able to learn how to navigate conversations to more in-depth conversational topics that are much more meaningful.

But one has to first learn how to navigate and read the situation before bringing up certain "heavier" type topics such as politics, religion, social issues, etc. The most important point is if a person is a good conversationalist and an active listener, people will tend to be more responsive to the individual and enjoy their company. This in turn could result in a person having more friends and a very successful study abroad experience.

WHY CURRENT EVENTS?

When you ask Asian students about what they talk about with their friends on an everyday basis, they usually say television shows, movie celebrities, music, food, fashion, sports, and maybe celebrity stars gossip. This is typical of what young people and students in any country talk about. In the US and in western countries, students generally speak about the very same topics. However, in addition, Americans and other westerners in general like to talk and discuss about other more in-depth and sometimes controversial topics like politics, religion, economics, world problems, social issues, environment, immigration, etc.

That is why for foreign students it is very important to prepare and know as much about the world happenings and US current events before arriving in the US. If an individual wants to be part of the conversations in the US with Americans and other foreign student friends, you will need to be up to date on what is happening in the US and the rest of the world.

It would be good practice to regularly read the international section from an English language newspaper printed in your country for the content and vocabulary regarding current events. If you don't always have the time to read the English language newspapers, it would still be beneficial to read the international section of the local newspaper in your language on a daily basis, as knowing and understanding the current and world events content is what is important.

WHY CURRENT EVENTS?

It would also be a good idea for you to watch and read news from stations like CNN or BBC or Al Jazeera. They give the most comprehensive coverage of the news of the world, the US, UK, and the Middle East and can offer an individual different perspectives that your home country news programs may not provide. Magazines such as the American Economist also go into much more depth and analysis of world issues, but magazines printed in the English language can be expensive and difficult to read and thereby, more challenging.

Every student should also understand about world politics and your country's role and relationship with the US. It would also help you to know about how, in general, Americans view your country and its international policies. Moreover, as a student, you should also be prepared to answer questions that will be asked about how your country views the US and the overall geopolitics of the region your country is located in. You will need to be able to explain more complex world issues in a logical and clear manner in English. If people cannot understand your English or follow your thought processes or understand the logic that is being applied, then you will be unable to effectively share with others about your thinking and point of view.

So long before you leave your home country for study abroad, it is advisable to have kept up with the current news by having read the newspapers about international and current events and looked up on the internet accurate information about the images that Americans have of your country. The reason is that these types of topics and questions will often be asked of you when you get to the US.

You should think of yourself as being an "ambassador" for your country because you may be one of the few or the first person from your country that some American students and other international students will meet and/or will ever get to know.

Thus, you should make every effort to make a favorable impression and what you say and how you say things are very important. How well a person relates to others is more than just the content but also how favorable an impression one can make in explaining things coherently, logically, and clearly in English.

> *"I get by with a little help from my friends."*
>
> *-Beatles-*

MAKING FRIENDS

Perhaps one of the most difficult but unexpected challenges for foreign students on study abroad programs in the US is making friends with Americans. You would think that since Americans are generally known to be outgoing and friendly that it would be easy to make friends in the US. But when I asked some Asian students about what was the biggest challenge for them when studying in the US, besides mastering the English language, the majority of respondents identified the issue of making American friends. Now logically not having strong English skills would make it difficult to make friends if you could not communicate effectively. Just using gestures and smiling and laughing will get old very fast for most Americans. So, first you must be able to speak and communicate proficiently in English and secondly, it is about cultural norms, common interests, and expectations.

I was just recently in Malaysia on one of my university visits. During the visit I met a Malaysian student who was proficient in English and studying in the US at a university in Ohio for a year and a half, but had to suddenly return home for a family emergency. I asked him what was the biggest challenge for him in the US and just like the Japanese students, he said "Making friends with Americans." I asked him to explain why. He said that he was a "night owl" who stayed up late and there weren't many American students to hang out with late at night. I asked him why it was difficult because there must have been some American students who stayed up late. He added that the US culture was different, the food and religion were different, and although interests were sometimes similar, there were still some difficulties in connecting and making good friends.

Consequently, I was very surprised that this student from Malaysia who was proficient in English had a difficult time making friends in the US. In the end, he said he hung out with the other international students, not Americans. I think it would be natural and easier for foreign students to hang out with other foreign students because they are going through similar experiences, including the challenges with the language and the culture. And that is fine for some of the time, but that is not the reason you go to America to study.

It could have been that the American students already had their friends on campus or they may have wanted to stay with students who were culturally similar to them, joke like them, and know the same expressions and "Americanisms." Therefore, unless the American students make an extra effort to get to know foreign students which is not always the case, then making connections and friendships with American students will require the foreign student to be more assertive, friendly and good at "small talk!"

Now of course, it could depend on what type of personality and character someone has since a more outgoing extroverted person would logically have an easier time making friends compared to a more quiet, introverted person. But the problem of making friends is not only experienced by foreign students in the US. It is a universal problem whenever individuals throughout the world meet.

At the university in Osaka where I was the Director of the International Center, we had over 100 international students and throughout the year, the number one complaint was that it was difficult to make friends with the Japanese students! So here was the exact opposite situation. Americans and other international students were coming to study in Japan and they were also having a difficult time making Japanese friends. It was similar to the situation in the US but where the Americans, who were the foreigners, usually ended up "hanging out" with the other international students. So, by looking at both examples in the US and Japan, I think we can conclude that it is not only about language but cultural differences, lifestyle preferences, personal expectations, maturity level, and/or areas of common interests.

Therefore, the focus on making friends should be at the top of the priority list for new incoming foreign and international students. That is why it is so important that from the very first day you arrive on campus, you must assert yourself into situations that will take you out of your normal comfort zone. It may mean that you will have to smile more and say hello and introduce yourself to everyone you meet.

When all the foreign and international students arrive on campus, they are all in the "same boat," as are the American students who are incoming freshmen or new transfers. Thus, especially during international student orientation activities or similar types of events, this is the ideal time that every student attending will normally have their guard down and be open to speaking with anyone. It's about just arriving on campus, the newness of the environment, everyone being in a similar situation, and sharing that same bit of awkwardness when you don't know anyone and are meeting people for the very first time. Make an effort to smile more, introduce yourself, start a "small talk" conversation, and look for topics of mutual interest. This may be the best first chance to start meeting new people and establishing friendships.

You may be jet lagged or tired from listening to English, but this is the best time to be extra outgoing and introduce yourself to as many other students, staff and teachers as possible to try and lay the foundation for future potential relationships. Relationships usually are developed when individuals have at least one common experience that both participants can relate to and talk about as a starting point to get more meaningful conversations going.

But also don't expect to have instant friendship resulting from these "one shot" types of events which are normally designed more as "ice breaker" types of activities to get people introduced and engaging. Later you can follow up on some of these initial introductions, regardless of how brief they might have been, to work on building friendships with people that you connected well with at the initial meeting.

At that point, it may just take a statement like "I remember meeting you at the orientation meeting," that potentially opens the door for a longer, more in-depth conversation about any mutual subject or the person's background, interests, etc. The key to developing friendships relationship can be started by the one deemed the "foreigner" having to take the initiative to try to make things happen. If one does not take the initiative to get things started, there is often the tendency for nothing to develop, as far as relationships are concerned. Especially for Americans, there most likely will be far more of them at the institutions than there will be foreign students, so they potentially have a much larger pool to interact with other Americans like themselves, rather than going out of their way to befriend foreign students.

Moreover, Americans may be more cautious approaching and taking the initiative with foreign students because they may not feel so comfortable that they know about the "do's" and "don'ts" of a foreign country's culture. So, they may hold back in taking the initiative to start a conversation.

The initial orientation and welcome activities can be a good beginning for campus life, but a foreign student must continue to take the initiative beyond that. Taking the initiative means putting oneself in a situation where conversations can arise naturally on areas of common interests. For example, attending sporting events, student plays and performances, campus club meetings, or even meetings off campus within the local community may provide opportunities to expand an individual's reach to other people with similar interest areas. This kind of exposure greatly heightens the prospects of meeting new people and developing friendships.

Believe me, once you have good friends to hang out with and a support system, your study abroad life will become enjoyable, fun, and exciting. However, it all has to start somewhere and you have to be willing to take the risk and initiative to leave your normal comfort zone to make things happen.

But remember as I wrote earlier, Americans won't necessarily understand your dilemma about struggling with the English language and also that some cultures like in Asia tend to be more reserved and shy. Since most American students may not know this, they may not take the initiative to come over and talk with foreign students. They may not know what to talk about or maybe it is just too much trouble for them. Remember most Americans have very little experience outside of the US.

In these cases, the foreign students must be the ones to take the risks to reach out to the American students. I know it is not really fair because in places like Asia, Asian people are usually exceptionally kind and hospitable to foreigners. But in the US, since America is so diverse, you will be treated just like everyone else. Many Americans may not know you are a foreign student. So don't expect any special attention except possibly from some

American students who may have gone on study abroad programs and have walked in your shoes, so they know the feeling and difficulties of being a foreigner and an outsider.

These types of students would be the best to initially make friends with because there are similar shared experiences which both individuals can relate to and talk about. If there are American students who have studied abroad or traveled to your country, they would be the easiest and most interested in making friends with you. Especially if the university teaches the language of your country, there should be numerous things of common interest to include in any conversation. In this case, there may also be several other American students who would love to meet you and be friends. Many returning American students, if they had a very good overseas experience, will want to give something back because they had such a good time in your country or region.

The only downfall here is that the American students who have studied in, say China or Japan and returned to the home campus, will probably want to speak and practice Chinese or Japanese with students from these two countries. And the Chinese or Japanese student while being in the US would want to speak English so that he/she can improve their English. So, some sort of compromise will need to be worked out as to what language will be used and how both languages will be given fair time. But normally the stronger language will always conquer. So if your English is better than the American student's Chinese language proficiency, then most likely the English language will be used most of the time, and visa versa.

To summarize, if a foreign student's objective is to make friends and get to know as many people as one can from the very first day on campus, the student must be prepared to be the one to initiate conversations. Once an international student has a close circle of friends, his/her entire campus life will change from feeling lonely and out of place, to being happier with greater satisfaction of the study abroad experience. The objective is to challenge yourself to get out of your dorm room, smile a lot, and say "hello" to as many people as possible on campus! Get involved with various student organizations on campus, joining student clubs, playing on the school sports teams, and just always be ready and open to new experiences and meeting new people. Also, remember that friendships begin with conversations and if others are reluctant to get the conversation going, it becomes your responsibility to try to give it a "kick start" to build meaningful and productive relationships.

> *"Keep your face to the sunshine and you cannot see a shadow."*
>
> -Helen Keller-

BEING POSITIVE

Needless to say, staying positive is always the ideal goal. It is only natural, especially when you are studying abroad that things can and occasionally will get a person down. It could be that you don't understand what the instructor is saying in class, you have so much homework that you cannot complete everything, you might not have many friends for an effective support network, you might miss speaking your home country language, or eating authentic food from your country. You may also miss your boyfriend or girlfriend or your mother and/or a father, and the list can go on and on.

One should anticipate that the initial struggle and transition after arriving on campus could be very difficult. You may go into culture shock. For many students, culture shock is very real. It can make people depressed, become negative, constantly prone to complaining, and just wanting to hide away in their room and sleep or always Skype with their boyfriend/girlfriend or mother/father. Culture shock affects people in different ways. Everyone reacts differently to a study abroad experience so there is no standard remedy to fit every situation. Anticipate that in general, the first two or three weeks after you arrive in the US will be the "honeymoon stage," where everything is wonderful and everything is so exciting and fun. You LOVE America! Then classes start and you might start to encounter culture shock. Culture shock can normally last from 3-4 weeks to two months. It's almost like being on information and emotional overload as one attempts to adjust to a new environment, new routines, new rules and standards, new ways of thinking and behaving, etc.

But once you get through the initial culture shock period, the satisfaction curve rises and eventually you reach a level of stability and confidence where you know that things will be okay. From that point on, you will start to enjoy the study abroad experience increasingly more and more. The human being is an amazing creature in that it has the innate ability to fine tune adjustments to fit a new environment or experience. There are a few students who will not experience any culture shock, but that is not the norm.

An individual will probably need to recognize that he/she can make the necessary adjustments to the new environment. However, one must work on developing effective strategies and different behaviors and ways of viewing things that may not have been necessary in one's home country. It sometimes may be helpful to talk with others who might be going through the same culture shock experience or who had experienced it and could work their way through it.

The important thing is to try to stay as positive as possible and always remember that "One may experience the darkest of the night before being able to eventually see the brightness of the sun." In the meantime, it may also be helpful that no matter how difficult things can get, to remain positive and "fake it until you can make it."

"A ship in a harbor is safe, but that is not what ships are built for."
-William G.T. Shedd-

RISK TAKING

Risk taking is an essential quality to becoming a successful leader, entrepreneur, and visionary. Entrepreneurs are usually risk takers. They have to be. If not, they would most likely not have started a new business, which is one of the riskiest things to do.

Generally, there are two types of risk taking. One type of "risk taking" is the decision to proceed with an action without any consideration of possible consequences. For example, to drive at 60 miles per hour on city streets to get to a destination faster may simply be "risk taking." Very little thought goes into thinking about the possible consequences such as having an accident or getting stopped by the police or creating a dangerous scenario for oneself and others who might also be present on the same streets as one's route. However, people often take the risk of driving too fast with little thought to possible consequences.

The other type of risk taking is called "calculated risk taking." In "calculated risk taking," as many possible variables, both positive as well as negative ones, are consciously thought through as possible outcomes if one took the contemplated action. Using the same driving scenario, if one considered the possible results and consequences of the contemplated action, most drivers would consider driving 60 miles per hour on city streets not a very logical choice and not worth the possible risks.

In this book, when there is reference to risk taking, it is the "calculated risk taking" that is being used as a reference point. Sometimes an individual can get away with plain and simple "risk taking," but the odds for success often go way down in comparison to engaging in "calculated risk taking."

In Asia, depending on the country, risk taking levels differ. In places like Japan, there is a tendency to usually be risk adverse. There is often a tendency to prefer the safe and stable path without much thought to looking at the larger picture. Avoiding risk tends to conform with societal expectations that the stability of the status quo is preferable to possibly disrupting things. The risk taking level of a country can be correlated to entrepreneurship. As an example, Japan ranks low on risk taking and consequently, it is also globally ranked low in entrepreneurship.

The Japanese are excellent at taking ideas which others had already taken the risk to pursue and then making subsequent refinements to improve the innovative product. One of the best examples is the development of the crystal mechanism in watch making, which was initially begun by the Swiss before the Japanese decided to take it a step further. The Japanese took the idea after it was introduced to become, at one time, one of the leaders in the further development and manufacturing of crystal mechanisms in most watches. However, today many people believe that the Japanese invented the crystal mechanism in watches, which is not true. In other areas of Asia like Hong Kong and Taiwan, there is a very strong risk taking spirit and therefore entrepreneurship is usually the norm in taking risks to start a new business to try and get ahead.

It is also evident that even as the global work force is continually evolving, where the English language and global life skills are required to stay competitive, the number of Japanese students going on study abroad programs to the US has dropped by 50% within the past 12 years. In contrast, other countries of the world are increasing their respective levels of participation in study abroad programs.

Studying abroad can be a big risk. If you are willing to pursue a study abroad program experience, then you are definitely a risk taker. Hopefully, your decision was a result of engaging in "calculated risk taking," rather than in simple "risk taking." One of the ways of characterizing the study abroad opportunity is that it can be one of the most exciting, scary, tension-filled, enjoyable, difficult, risky, and wonderful experiences of an individual's life.

Andre Glide said, "Man cannot discover new oceans unless he has the courage to lose sight of the shore." Please remember, dangerous or reckless risk taking is not what is being suggested here. I am talking about carefully thought out calculated risk taking that has the greater chance of making a person successful and greatly improving one's quality of life.

"The true sign of intelligence is not knowledge but imagination."

-Albert Einstein-

CREATIVITY

Perhaps the one quality of America that many foreign students who have studied in the US have been impressed by is the creative and innovative environment of the US. Many foreign students have expressed how creative Americans can be, how the learning systems and education encourages creative thinking on how to do things and solve problems to reach one's full potential. I think the exposure to the creative aspect of the US on the university campuses will definitely have a huge impact on foreign students because many foreign university educational systems do not usually focus on creativity and originality, but more on following tradition and what has already been done before.

In many countries, there is not the constant critical thinking of how can we do this better or how can we continually improve this system. Due to many countries having large populations, long histories, the need for control, the hierarchical structure, the relationship obligations and the very time tested way of doing things, young people usually don't question their "senpai" (senior) or teachers. The belief usually is the older a person is, the wiser the person should be.

The challenge for many educational systems in the world, say for example in Japan, is that the present educational system does not encourage or challenge people to think creatively. And this is where study abroad to the US will really open up this potential to learn and experience what true creativity is all about.

Just look at the Ted Talks on You Tube that have been around for over 30 years. There are hundreds of educational programs and really great ideas presented on the Ted Talks on the internet. To me, the Ted Talks are the best example of why the US is the leader at sharing and exchanging original and innovative ideas. And if you listen closely to some of the best speakers of the Ted Talks, it can really get you excited about new discoveries and creative ways of doing things.

The US is really the ideal location for creativity, being original, and generating excitement for developing new ways of doing things. That is why Silicon Valley is in the US, and where Apple, Facebook, Twitter, and other social media were all born–where Disneyland and Universal Studios, multimedia productions and Hollywood movies all began. Even the music and fashion industry trends usually start in the US. The US offers international students the opportunity to dream and think big, there is no one saying that you cannot do something or you cannot be somebody. And even if someone says you can't, you don't have to listen to them and can do it anyway!

Other western countries also do offer similar opportunities to be openly creative and free, but none do it to the scale and to the degree that the US does. Part of it is size and population, part of it is the American way and mindset, and part of it is the history and education system of the US. And that is why I suggest that if you can afford to attend a university or college in the US, to please do so. The US is really like no other country in the world.

And I am not saying that everything in the US is so great, but in certain areas like creative freedom, originality, innovation, and so many opportunities, the US is second to none. And this is where foreign students can really be inspired to reach their full creative potential. Dan Pink, a famous author and speaker on Ted Talks, said that what we need to motivate people is "autonomy, mastery, and purpose." Study abroad is the perfect platform to offer foreign students the chance to achieve these three things during their study abroad experience in the US.

"Everything is funny, as long as it's happening to someone else."

-Will Rogers-

SENSE OF HUMOR

A sense of humor will differ and vary greatly between cultures. It usually will reflect culture, society and popular culture, and is one of the most difficult things for a non-English speaking foreign student to understand. In American culture, there are several different kinds and levels of humor, from slapstick to black humor. Americans also like to use sarcasm in much of their humor. Sarcasm is not common in most Asian languages so it may be difficult to follow and understand for second language learners.

For example, Americans may say something with a straight face that you may take seriously, but they are actually only joking. But after a couple of seconds, you can usually tell by the other person's face if they were joking or not. Nevertheless, it may take some time to understand and become accustomed to what is considered funny and constitutes the sense of humor of Americans.

Many Americans like to be funny whenever they can. They are many times the mood makers at parties or social functions, many of whom are talkative, and they really enjoy teasing one another and joking around. Some Americans are always joking around and it's often hard to know when they are serious. I know it's sometimes awkward when you are with American friends, especially in a group setting, and someone says something supposedly funny and everyone laughs. And you might just laugh along to be part of the group, but you may not have any idea of what was so funny.

SENSE OF HUMOR

It's also very uncomfortable when someone makes a joke or teases you and you don't know what is so funny, but everyone around you is laughing. And you don't know if they are laughing at you or at the joke or both. It's a very uncomfortable and embarrassing feeling when this happens. But this is all part of the study abroad experience and it will make you much sharper and more inclined to pay close attention to what people are saying because you want to be part of the group and understand what they are talking about.

To be able to freely joke successfully in the English language with Americans will take a lot of time. First, humor is very difficult to understand in another culture without the cultural and social background and history. Second, trying to be funny in your own language is difficult enough, but in a second language, it is extremely difficult without knowing all of the words, slangs, background, and expressions. And third, Americans usually speak very fast, often times not in complete sentences, and for someone not raised in the US, some American's sense of humor can seem quite odd and strange at times.

It is also very important to understand that the US is not a homogeneous country. It is comprised of a variety of ethnic groups, not all with the same history and backgrounds. So within certain groups, a topic that is common and perfectly acceptable among members of the "in-group" may be viewed as inappropriate when used by someone who is not considered part of the "in-group." For example, a person of Jewish heritage might not be offended if another person of Jewish background uses the term "Jew" to describe someone of a similar background. Because the word "Jew" has mostly negative stereotypical connotations, it is often more politically correct to use the word "Jewish" heritage, background, or upbringing to describe someone of that group. Nevertheless, it might be more acceptable for a person of Jewish heritage to use the term with another person of the same faith who does not use the term with any negative connotation.

The same concept may also apply, especially for ethnic-specific terms, to other ethnic groups in the US. This is what is called "In-group, Out-group." If you are part of the "in-group", you can make jokes or say things that people who are not from your in-group (out-group) should not say. If the "out-group" person did say something that only an "in-group" person can say, then many times the "in-group" people would get very upset at the "out-group" person.

You see this often in the US. It may be among ethnic groups, sometimes regarding gender or orientation, and other times people who have shared a certain emotional experience together. For example, soldiers who have faced combat duty would potentially be the "in-group," compared to other soldiers who have not yet seen combat duty (out-group).

Keep in mind that in the US, there are many jokes made about other ethnic groups and are generally to make fun by putting down that group or emphasizing generally negative stereotypes about the group. It is not politically correct, but it's sometimes part of American humor and sarcasm–making fun of others and their differences. You will need to filter your assessment and make good judgments about its appropriateness or inappropriateness because what is acceptable or not acceptable can often shift depending on who you are talking to.

My advice would be not to try and joke with Americans about any subject that is related to other ethnic groups or stereotypes and stay on positive types of humor that do not put down ethnic groups, customs or differences. Remember joking in another language is extremely difficult and there are very sensitive nuances and hidden meanings. Some foreign students may want to try to be part of the joking exchange but without knowing enough, the individual may sometimes cross the line of what is considered unacceptable and hurt someone's feelings. That is not where you want to go. So keep things positive and don't participate when other's are saying negative types of jokes or putdowns about other ethnicities or people.

Along the same lines, some of the jokes you will hear are called "inside jokes" meaning that you have to be part of the small, inner core of people who know the background information to understand the joke. Often times even other Americans who are not part of the core group would not understand what is so funny. In these cases, don't worry about trying to figure out what was so funny because you probably won't have enough information and the joke is probably insignificant to anyone outside the "inner group".

One more important note regarding joking styles in the US. Some Americans also like to covertly disguise or make a "play on words," regarding sex, body parts, and sexuality. This is especially common more among American male university students. It is usually not blatant and is often a carefully coded innuendo so it could mean different things to different people. But fellow Americans will understand right away when another American makes a "play on words" which are sexually connoted or a nuance meaning is implied. Some people may laugh, others may take offense and many just don't pay attention. These types of jokes will take a long time to grasp, so don't worry if you don't understand what is supposed to be so funny. I think this type of joking is somewhat an "American thing."

In summary, it will take time for you to be able to learn how to effectively joke with Americans. But the day you can joke with Americans in the English language, that will be a major milestone because being funny in a second language is unbelievably difficult as it requires a combination of knowing the vocabulary, expressions and language; understanding the context; and the sense of humor that is usually culturally or socially based. But just give it some time, pay close attention, and eventually you will start to understand the sense of humor of Americans. And soon after, you may be the one making the jokes and teasing the Americans in English. And that will be a major benchmark!

"If it doesn't challenge you, it won't change you."

MOTIVATION

When you are studying abroad, there will be many times that you will be overwhelmed and feel unmotivated and won't feel like doing anything. You may be on overload about the new study abroad life in the US. Maybe you don't feel like going to class or you don't feel like going to study at the library. Many people who are not feeling up to doing something or are unmotivated may say something like "I don't feel like it," and not do anything.

Action doesn't usually follow feeling, feeling follows action. In the US, there is an expression, "Fake it until you make it." This means that even if a person doesn't feel like doing something or going somewhere, the person will still get out of bed, get dressed and go out to do what the individual originally didn't feel like doing. And gradually by "faking it," the person usually starts to feel better about doing what he/she resisted and eventually feels more and more satisfied about accomplishing something instead of lying in bed all day. And as long as you continue this pattern of taking positive action even if you don't feel motivated at all, eventually a deeper motivation will return and then student life will become much easier to navigate again. A possible truism would be when an individual doesn't feel like doing something, maybe doing the unpleasant something is exactly the thing to do!

MOTIVATION

The driver or inner source of energy to keep you moving forward is called "motivation." It is a distinguishing characteristic of most human beings that defines each of us. It is what generally separates the "haves" from the "have nots." The "haves" usually have a lot of motivation to do things. The "have nots" usually have little reason of doing more than the bare minimum that might be required.

Motivation is created by having a vision or idea or feeling of what something will look or feel like when an objective or goal is reached. Sometimes we have to use an emotionally charged feeling that a movie or music or love gives us that helps motivate us to keep pushing forward towards our goal. But without a concrete "vision," motivation is generally weak.

Many times, we just dream about something which does not usually evolve into a true "vision" of an objective or goal to be intently pursued. "Dreaming" is more about just wishful thinking with no follow up action while having a "vision" is more about taking specific action and having concrete incremental steps to get to an objective.

Take study abroad as an example. It should not be a "dream," but rather a concrete "vision" of a better life for oneself. However, it should not end up as a "what" but rather a "how" to get to the vision or goal. And there will be unexpected bumps in the road, like every plan in life because nothing ever works out exactly like originally imagined. There will be starts and stops, happiness and disappointments, and opportunities and setbacks.

Realistically, a study abroad student should be prepared for all of these things possibly happening on the journey to achieve the ultimate goal–a successful study abroad experience resulting in achieving objectives such as a good paying job, a more exciting and promising work career, or a life-changing experience, etc. In addition, in a highly competitive world, individuals who are more motivated will usually do whatever they are required to do to achieve success in attaining their vision. The less motivated an individual may be, the chances are proportionately diminished. So if an individual keeps the "vision" in front of him/herself and uses it to continually motivate oneself, the chances for success are far greater than someone who does not truly have a clear vision.

The more an individual can connect motivation to personal commitment, the greater the possibility of reaching one's goal. Pressure imposed from the outside of a person is usually not as strong a driver as one feeling personally committed to the goal. Ideally, the more personal and internalized the goal, the higher the motivation and the better the chances are of overcoming obstacles and setbacks.

Nonetheless, motivation is only half of the equation for success. People may say that they are very motivated, but if there is no follow-up action, very little or no progress will be made toward the ultimate objective. One should act by using the motivation and converting it into productive behavior and action that advances one toward achieving the objective.

For instance, you may sincerely believe that there is a need to improve your English language proficiency to be successful on a study abroad program, but if you do not do anything more than just think about it, there will be no change in your language proficiency. However, if you are motivated enough to take English language classes at a local private English language school or find a native English language tutor or start listening to English language programs on a daily basis to become more familiar with the language, then the motivation and follow-up action will help you to advance closer to your ultimate goal.

Motivation and follow-up action go hand in hand and very often will determine how well a student will do on a study abroad program. If the reason to be motivated can be internalized by the student, the greater the chances for success. However, if the reason is "owned" mainly by the parents, the drive and follow-up action will not be shared to the same extent by the student.

For an investment as large as a study abroad experience with all the costs, sacrifices, time, and effort, the student needs to be strongly motivated. Personal motivation is the key and not just because the parents want the student to go. This difference of who "owns" the motivation can be the difference between success and failure. And if you allow someone else's motivation to be your reason for attending a study abroad program, once the "honeymoon" period is over, you may find yourself just doing the minimum to satisfy the requirements of that moment, rather than to truly excel and try to reach one's full potential.

Of course, staying motivated all the time is never easy. And there may be times that you don't feel motivated at all. So when the difficult challenges come and you don't feel motivated to do anything, then just "fake it until you make it" until your deeper inner motivation returns.

> *"Satisfaction of one's curiosity is one of the greatest sources of happiness in life."*
>
> *-Linus Pauling-*

BEING CURIOUS

I understand that it is an unusual request to suggest to someone to be more curious. Most people think that you cannot control your level of curiosity. It is also often assumed that it is already part of your character or your nature and a person is either the curious type or not. But I believe a person can and should become more and more curious if he/she chooses to do so.

If a person is interested and excited about life, the individual is more apt to be curious about many things such as why things happen as they do, how could we improve the situation, what would happen if things were different, etc. Being curious is one of the best ways to expand your horizons and discover things that you never knew before.

It is very important to be observant, notice and be aware of things, and when you are uncertain about something, to seek an answer. You should be willing to ask questions to help you know and understand things better. This is how many people increase their knowledge and understanding and it opens up doors to meet people and make friends. It's really that simple.

Being curious about things is about wanting to know more about everything in life. Being curious is wondering why certain things are the way they are. It is the first step in being a critical thinker. Most critical thinkers are curious people who wonder why things are as they are and how could they improve or make it better. Sometimes the word "curious" is associated with being "nosy," which has a negative meaning. Another example of a negative meaning of being curious is the proverb "Curiosity killed the cat!" which implies negative consequences to one being curious.

There is nothing wrong with being curious if the questions asked are appropriate and asked in the right way and tactfully timed. Being curious is also the first step to being a good conversationalist. Asking interesting and related questions will help "lubricate" the conversation and people will usually be happy to talk about something that they are familiar with. So being observant and curious and then asking good questions will potentially help you in all areas of academics, social skills, making friends, and being a good conversationalist.

If you are a study abroad student in the US and people know that you are a foreign student, they would expect that you would want to know more about the US and Americans in general. And as was mentioned before, most people like to talk about things that are familiar to them. Anything having to do with the US is usually a familiar topic to them and many people will be happy to share their opinions with you.

There is a saying which goes something like "Know what you know, but more importantly, know what you don't know." It is also very important that a foreign student not pretend that he/she knows something when one actually doesn't really know. My advice is if you don't know–ask about it. Likewise, by being curious and initially asking a lot of questions, it may be the best way to gain a deeper sense of things and why things are happening as they are.

Most people assume that they know, but they may actually not know things to the extent they believe they know because their knowledge level may be only a superficial understanding of the topic. Don't be surprised if one finds some Americans like this, where the knowledge base is "a mile wide, but only an inch thick."

In short, you should be as curious as you want to be and consider curiosity as one of the essential tools to increase your knowledge base, experiences, and understanding of things in the US.

"Spontaneity is the best kind of adventure."

SPONTANEITY AND IMPROVISATION

I think that foreign students will find that American students are very good at being spontaneous and quick to improvise. I think it is related to being a quick thinker and decision maker, which I also believe is part of

SPONTANEITY AND IMPROVISATION

critical thinking and problem solving. In classes, for presentations, role playing, skits and other types of semi-performance activities, Americans tend to be very good at "winging it," which means just doing the activity without much preparation or serious thought. Basically, you are figuring things out at the same moment you are actually trying to perform or do the activity. This concept incorporates being spontaneous and being good at improvising.

Someone who is spontaneous is someone who can suddenly come up with some idea or action that often is done suddenly at a time when no one expects it. In other words, being spontaneous is to take unexpected risk/action at the spur of the moment.

For example, if someone just suddenly got up and started to dance to the music at some event when no one else was dancing, this would fit the concept of spontaneous behavior. The word spontaneous is usually associated with someone who is original and fresh, literally someone who is doing something that is totally unexpected.

Spontaneity would be something that would be probably frowned upon in many Asian countries and cultures. In the US, spontaneous behavior can also be discouraged at formal events that require formality and uniformity. But in informal situations, Americans who are spontaneous and funny are usually popular and well liked. They are willing to take risks and do things at the spur of the moment.

Both spontaneous and improvisation requires someone who is quick thinking and creative. The word "improvise" means to quickly come up with an idea to cover something when it is not going well. Americans also admire people who can "think on their feet." This phrase refers to people who can problem solve and think quickly while something is happening and they are capable of quickly changing something to make some improvement. The American TV series called "Whose Line is it Anyway?"

is the best example of improvisation and spontaneity. If you want to see the most unbelievable talent of combining all three skills of improvisation, spontaneity, and sense of humor into one show, watch the old reruns of this American TV program.

This idea to improvise would not really be understood by most Asian students because in many Asian cultures, one tends not to change something all of a sudden. One is normally expected to follow the schedule or plan and do what is expected until the end. Being good at improvising would not be looked at in a positive way in many Asian cultures. That is because it is the exact opposite of what many Asian cultures tend to emphasize, that one should prepare well and be completely ready. If a person had to improvise, it would normally mean that one was not prepared, which is probably true in most cultures.

Americans occasionally will say, "Let's just wing it," when they haven't prepared enough and don't have any more time. Many times the "winging it" is related to doing a presentation or a skit or some kind of project that involves a performance or being in front of people. It is hard to "wing" a term paper or quiz or test. So "winging it" in America is usually related to some class project or oral presentation that many Americans may feel that they can get by using their wit and humor and ability to improvise.

For many foreign students, especially those from Asia where "winging it" would never be considered acceptable behavior, this nonchalant type of attitude would be nerve wracking and very difficult since improvising means a person might not know exactly what the other people will be doing or saying, but one has to respond or react with something.

Furthermore, if an individual is a second language learner, to be expected to figure out things as they are happening live in front of an audience and then to respond appropriately would be the worst nightmare due to possible nuances in the language while at the same time having to think up something creative or funny to say on the spot. It would be the highest level of stress for foreign students who are still struggling with English.

But if you really look closely at this type of situation, it takes a very talented person to "wing it" in appropriate situations and still do a good job. So the better an individual can become at being spontaneous and being able to skillfully improvise in the US, the more exciting one's study abroad experience may become. And if an individual can become very good at it, other Americans will respect that ability.

Combining the creative nature of many Americans with spontaneity and improvisation is why Americans, in general, are often very good at coming up with fresh ideas on doing imaginative skits, talent shows, and performances.

So carefully observe other American students who are spontaneous, as well as those who can improvise in various situations. Learn from these observations and try to gradually experiment if you want to. But remember, there are social and cultural norms and cues, and sometimes being spontaneous walks the fine line of potentially being socially accepted and funny or being thought of as strange or inappropriate. So one should always weigh the value of being spontaneous versus sticking to the script. I would strongly suggest that a person watch very carefully and study people who are known to be spontaneous or good at improvising and learn from them as to what is socially accepted and appropriate.

> *"To find yourself, think for yourself."*
> -Socrates-

INDEPENDENT THINKER

Americans usually pride themselves on being independent thinkers. That is one of the reasons why the US is viewed as a heterogeneous and diverse country. People who have opinions are usually able to explain why they think something is right or wrong, using logic or data or emotion or some kind of reference. That is why Americans and westerners, in general, like to discuss politics, economics, religion, current events, and social issues. They have been taught ever since they were very young to think for themselves and to have opinions about things, even if sometimes their opinions are not correct or they are opposite of what the government or society's stance might be.

Independent thinking has created a situation where there is constant churning because people are exploring "what ifs," as part of their independent thinking. People are interested in exploring and possibly trying new options to long held beliefs. This has led to greater creativity and new innovations. When this happens, it tends to be positive as improvements take place throughout society and generally helps people. However, like anything positive which is pushed to an extreme, sometimes a positive can also turn into being more of a negative.

Independent thinking may fall into that category when there is a lack of consensus on a variety of social, political, and economic issues because everyone has their own set ideas or opinions about an issue. Study abroad students should be prepared to anticipate facing this dilemma when there appears to be no consensus on an issue. Inquiring with one person may produce one response, while addressing the same issue with others may result in possibly as many different responses as the number of people asked. It is important to understand this when it happens.

It doesn't necessarily mean that only one individual's response is completely correct, but it may be more a reflection of individuals having vastly different perspectives on the same issue due to their knowledge of the issue, experiences, or personal biases developed because of everyone being an independent thinker. This type of active, but sometimes inconclusive dialogue, is also a part of the fabric of democracy in the US.

When a study abroad student encounters contrary or differing viewpoints on the same issue, it becomes very important for the student to examine the issue further and to come to an informed conclusion that makes the most sense to him/her. It is advisable to initially take information from others at "face value," but keeping in mind that more critical thinking or examination may be necessary because the information may not necessarily be totally accurate.

If one does not do this personal examination, one might later find that knowledge or beliefs assumed to be accurate and true may not be totally correct. Consequently, a small degree of skepticism in information obtained from individuals who have been raised to be independent thinkers may be best in guiding a foreigner's own understanding of things.

America is a democracy where individual freedom is really a very important right and people do take this right very seriously. However, sometimes I do think Americans are too free in the sense that someone is always protesting or complaining about something which sometimes leads to divisiveness within the group. I believe that an individual still has to also have the commitment and skills to be a team player to be successful. In my eyes, if I were a boss looking to hire the ideal employee, I would hire an "independent thinker who is also able to be a team player." These two qualities in the same person are the most important attributes for any truly global company or organization.

> *"Persuasion is often more effectual than force."*
>
> -Aesop-

SALES AND PERSUASION

On its face, oftentimes the word "sales" has a negative connotation. People think of someone trying to sell them something that they really don't want to buy. But I look at "sales" as part of everything we do. Teaching is a form of sales, talking with someone is basically sales in the form of persuasion. This book is a form of encouragement to study abroad which is a form of "sales" or persuasion. And anyone who has the ability to persuade other people through their story, logic, humor, knowledge, ability, or what other ways, is skilled at "sales."

So, the better "sales skills" you have, the more successful you could be and potentially have many more friends and acquaintances. Studying abroad in the US will help you to improve your ability to convince and persuade others because studying in the US requires students to debate, discuss, and persuade the teacher and other classmates through their written papers and oral presentations.

The Socratic method of teaching and learning–which includes critical thinking, questioning, discussion, debate, and persuasion are all part of the educational system in the US. Clarity, logic and English language proficiency are also necessary to convince and persuade others in the US. Consequently, the more comfortable and proficient you are with the English language, along with your logic and skills of persuasion, the greater the chances of you to engage and hold the interest of people and make the "sale."

"Expect Nothing and Appreciate Everything"

APPRECIATION

When you are studying abroad, no matter how difficult and trying your study abroad experience may be, throughout the entire experience you should never forget your parents, relatives, friends, seniors (senpai), and teachers/mentors who helped get you to where you are on your study abroad program. Sometimes when things are really difficult and we are faced with so much adversity and overwhelming challenges, we start to get into our own heads and start feeling sorry for ourselves.

It is at these times that we must always remember and never forget the basics of where we came from and who and what we should be grateful for. By always being mindful of being grateful and appreciative of what others have contributed to your life, often at great personal sacrifices. It will help you to maintain a healthy mind and heart to stay positive and to never give up.

People who are grateful are almost always happy and satisfied individuals because they tend to be very cognizant and sensitive in understanding the realities of life. Most are counting their blessings and not feeling sorry for themselves in terms of what they don't have or cannot do.

These types of people have a good understanding and acceptance of whatever they have in life and value them as precious assets. So always remember how fortunate you are to be able to have a study abroad experience. There are so many young people and students from your home country that would give anything to go on a study abroad program, especially to the US, but for whatever reason are unable to do so.

You will be experiencing a once in a lifetime opportunity that will change your future and life forever. You will see things, encounter new experiences, and meet diverse people that none of your friends and classmates who remained at home will ever experience. You are living the dream!

Commitment and hard work will get you through the struggles and hardships and only then will you understand that the process and journey are as important as reaching your final goal and destination. And once you get to the US, if you are not already there, I suggest you call your Dad and Mom today on Skype and thank them for sending you to the US for an unforgettable, life-changing experience!

"Change: If there is no struggle, there is no progress."

-Frederick Douglass-

THE STRUGGLE

Study abroad will be a life-changing event, but as we say in America, "There is no free lunch." This means that the opportunity and successful completion of the experience will not just be given to you because like most things in life, you must work hard and earn it. There is no quick and easy "instant gratification" to graduate or complete a program while studying abroad.

For you to reach a true level of accomplishment and satisfaction, you must be extremely committed to your goals and willing to give your all for it. To graduate from a US university in a second language will be a struggle that will compel you to push past what you thought were your farthest limits.

In the US, the overall percentage of students who drop out of a college or university can be an indicator of how difficult and rigorous a US university education can be. In fact, 53% of all enrolled students who began pursuit of a university degree in the US ended up dropping out and not achieving a degree. That equates to 47%, less than half of all students who start a college degree program in the US, will see the program all the way through to graduation. As they often say about US universities, it is much easier to be admitted "in" than to graduate "out."

So, that should give you a better perspective that if US domestic, native English speaking students struggle to get through college, then foreign students who speak English as a second or third language will have that much more of a challenge.

In contrast, in places like Japan, it is more difficult to get into a good university or college, but overall easier to graduate. Japan's college drop out percentage is only about 10%, which may look good from the stance of the universities doing a much better job of getting their students through college. But the more likely reason for such a low dropout percentage is that it is basically quite easy to graduate from a university in Japan without the same type of rigor that American universities require.

There is also a lot of pressure on the staff and faculty of a Japanese university to graduate as high a percentage of students as possible within four years, even in situations where sometimes the students who do not produce passable work will many times still be permitted to graduate with a degree.

Especially at the beginning of one's US study abroad experience, whether it be class lectures and assignments, the English language, daily life, or making friends, it can all be overwhelming at times. But it is the process and lessons of the "struggle" and learning to overcome the hardships that are the true "gems in the sand" that will help you to learn, grow, and move up to life's next level.

While you are in college and young, free, and flexible, it will be the best time for you to learn from your mistakes. As a well known study abroad consultant in Japan, Mr. Nobuyuki Suzuki, used to say to outbound Japanese students at his pre-departure presentations, "Trouble should be welcomed!" This meant that the true learning and personal development happens when there is trouble and struggle because most people are apt to learn more from their mistakes than from their successes.

If your study abroad experience turns out to be only fun and enjoyable the entire time you were on study abroad, you should ask for your money back because it is generally through the challenges, setbacks and the solving of problems and adversity, that you learn, mature, and grow.

Thus, after overcoming all the difficulties and trials of your study abroad experience, when you graduate you will experience the euphoric feeling of accomplishment, satisfaction and fulfillment that will far outweigh all the difficult times and tears that you put into your studies to graduate from an American university.

In short, the experience of studying abroad will have been priceless! And no one can ever take away your life-defining experiences, education, or degree, as well as that feeling of pride and accomplishment. And there is only one clear way to reach that level of satisfaction and achievement, by taking incremental steps as you learn from the experiences and struggles that you endured on the journey. And the biggest bonus is what you learn about yourself and who you really are.

"Life is largely a matter of expectation."
-Horace-

MANAGING EXPECTATIONS

A relative of mine once told me that the secret to managing people and organizations was in managing people's expectations. I believe that the same principle can be applied to study abroad programs and everything else in life. It's a psychological shift, a certain way of changing the way we perceive things. Managing expectations of yourself will help you to better cope with problems and disappointments. Doing so should mentally prepare you so you don't feel so overwhelmed or disappointed when things don't go according to your expectations.

Some students naively think of study abroad as a kind of vacation experience, but these expectations are very far removed from the actual reality. Certainly, many study abroad experiences include wonderful aspects that can be like a dream when things go well, but more often than not, there are struggles and adversity that one will have to overcome. And if you have managed your expectations correctly so that they are closer to the reality of your daily life situations, you will be able to handle those smaller bumps in the road quickly and move forward.

If you do not manage your expectations well, the gap between your expectations and the reality of the study abroad experience will be huge. That means that when things don't go your way, you will be overwhelmed or shocked because you did not adequately anticipate and prepare for what was coming.

If you do the necessary research and mental preparation prior to arrival in the US to keep your expectations as close as you can to the reality of the situation on the ground, you will have a much easier time assimilating and getting through the inevitable troubles that most foreign and international students first encounter.

Ideally, prior to departure, you have talked with someone from your home country who has already studied abroad. The individual doesn't necessarily have to have attended the same institution you will be attending. However, just understanding some of the realities of any study abroad program should give you a better sense of what could happen. That may be the best way to better understand what the experience and reality are all about.

A little bit of homework may be required to find someone from your home country who had a study abroad experience at the school or region you plan to attend. But that would be the best type of information to find out first-hand from the individual's personal experiences.

It is the same when you start working after graduation. If you can successfully manage your colleague's and supervisor's expectations of you, as well as your own expectations, you will have a much easier time and be much more successful and happy on the job. This may also mean that you must be very honest with yourself as to what your personal strengths and weaknesses are, what your preferences of choices are when they are presented as options, and moreover, if you have a candid and realistic understanding and acceptance of who you are and how others tend to see you. Once you better understand who you really are, it becomes easier to manage other people's expectations of you because you know what you can and cannot do.

In regards to studying abroad, prior to leaving you should also have as much information as you possibly can have about the study abroad country and the university, the student body, the history and culture, the university curricula, the student population, and the community around the university. The more you know about the new university the more mentally and emotionally prepared you will be when problems and challenges occur.

And so, when you first arrive on campus and face the inevitable surprises and challenges that come with most study abroad programs, they will not seem to be as daunting because you were mentally prepared and had done your homework prior to coming to the US. Therefore, through research, organized preparation, and managing your expectations, you will be more in control of your study abroad challenges and life in general.

> *"Don't worry about failures, worry about the chances you miss when you don't even try."*
>
> -Jack Canfield-

FAILING AND BUILDING CONFIDENCE

Initially, when you arrive in the United States and start classes, you can expect to be stressed out by the English requirements, the style of lecture and expected participation in classes, the amount of assignments and homework, the cultural differences, and you may not have the same confidence level that you had back in your home country.

When you were at home you may have been the smartest student in class or one of the best students in high school or college. But in the US, the environment and circumstances will have changed. Back home you may have been a "big fish in a small pond," but upon arrival in the US, you might feel more like a "small minnow in the vast ocean."

Studying abroad in another country and adjusting to a new language can be very humbling, but through the process of figuring things out and

FAILING AND BUILDING CONFIDENCE

overcoming challenges, you will gradually build your confidence and self-esteem to a much higher degree than when you left your native country. And the best way to regain and build confidence is to experience and take on as many challenges as you can while in the US. It is strongly recommended that you learn by doing and experiencing as much as possible.

More than textbook learning, it is the experiential learning that is important because it is much more practical and lasting. By opening yourself to examining and challenging whatever may be in front of you, you will start to realize that even if you were not good at something or even failed at times, it was okay because that's all part of life.

Hopefully, the failing is not in classes but even if this does happen, you may be able to either drop the class before the drop date deadline, if institution procedures and protocol allow such an option. If you received a very low grade, many universities will generally allow the student to retake the course and the most recent class grade will replace the earlier class grade. So hopefully, it will not hurt your GPA too much.

I believe that if you are honestly trying your best and if you are still not successful, that there are still very valuable lessons that can be learned by experiencing failures. I recall my own undergraduate experience where my major was environmental science and I needed to pass a chemistry course in order to meet the requirements to graduate. I had never had chemistry in high school and was terrible with numbers. So when I took chemistry, I was totally confused and just couldn't get it. I ended up dropping chemistry three different times which actually prolonged my graduation by a year.

At the time, I was young, just getting by in classes, and "cutting a lot of corners" but when I failed and had to drop chemistry three times, it really took its toll on my self-confidence and self-esteem. I felt that maybe I wouldn't be able to graduate from college. But I finally had to do a mindset shift and put all of my energy and concentration on my fourth try in taking the class. I had to just completely commit myself to going over every practice exercise in the text and spending hours every day to try and grasp the basic chemistry concepts.

And so I did every homework problem and read everything in the assigned chapters. As a result, on the fourth attempt, I was able to get a "B" grade and pass the course. I finally was able to prove to myself that I could do it if I seriously applied myself and followed through on what I was supposed to do. And that failure of chemistry would teach me that I can do almost anything, but it many times will require really hard work, determination, and commitment. The lesson I learned at that young age was that there was "no free lunch in life." And that lesson has kept me on track and has stayed with me until today.

In Google's eight innovation principles, #5 says "Never fail to fail." This is how great things come about, "Fail frequently, fail fast, and fail forward." Failing is part of the learning and if an individual is to fail, it is best to do as much of the failing as possible when an individual is still relatively young. Ideally, you don't want to go through these failing experiences when you are older and there might be more at stake, but determining when to experience failure is often not within the control of an individual.

The important thing to keep in mind is that failure can just be a step to eventual success and that one should take the opportunity to learn as much as possible from the experience. So be prepared to take on every challenge and expect that sometimes you will fail or not do well.

There will be other times when you will be successful, but either which way, you should be gaining invaluable experience and personal confidence just by challenging yourself. Ultimately, the most important lesson to be learned is that although failing is disappointing, you will survive and it should make you a better person because of the experience.

In many ways, you can actually learn more by failing than by always succeeding. But I am not saying that a person should deliberately try to fail, but if a person does fail, learn from it so it doesn't happen again, at least not by having to do it three more times like me!

"You must be the change you see in the world."
-Mahatma Gandhi-

DEALING WITH CHANGE

Thomas Boswell, noted *Washington Post* sports columnist, wrote in 1989 in his baseball book *The Heart of the Order* that "Either you change yourself or things change you. That's the choice." This quotation accurately captures what a study abroad experience can be all about.

Make no mistake about it. A study abroad experience is all about change. While you may be comfortable with your current situation because much of it is very familiar and you are in control, study abroad will take you to a totally different environment with unknown social mores and cultural expectations. Studying abroad is not for everyone, but it has tremendous potential for those who are more adventurous and want to improve themselves.

By first managing one's expectations that change is inevitable and will occur, one can be better prepared to take on the challenges that he/she will face while studying abroad. It may start with the realization that the most plausible of changes will be the development of coping strategies to deal with the new situations that you may be faced with for the first time in your life.

All too often, when change happens, people tend to believe that the situation will naturally change for the better to suit one's needs or that other people will change their undesirable behaviors to better meet your expectations. In all honesty, there is a very small percentage of this ever happening in either situation because change will most likely require you to change, rather than the other way around. By having the expectation that you will have to adjust to the change, you are ahead of the curve in first examining what behavior and thinking will have to take place to help you adjust to the change.

For example, since you will often be viewed in the US as an ethnic minority within the larger population of the US and there is little or nothing you can personally do to change that fact, one has several options to deal with the new change. One option would be denial, which would not be very productive since you cannot deny being an ethnic minority or change the country you come from. Moreover, simply changing the number of people in the ethnic minority group and the majority group are impossible unless conditions change radically.

Another option can be to try to assimilate within the larger population by adjusting where appropriate, your behavior and standards more towards that of the expectations and standards of the majority population. That requires you to be more conscious of your own behavior and how it may be perceived by others. Be congnizant of behavior which may have been acceptable in your native country but which may not be as acceptable in your new host environment.

Just by being more conscious of one's behavior will be a change for you because you probably never had to do this before. It requires an internal processing of new information under a different set of circumstances. Your engaging in the thought process alone will represent, for most study abroad students, a greater awareness of the need for change due to being in a different social and cultural environment.

The second step is to begin thinking, before one leaves the comfort of one's native country, about the range of possible personal changes which may be required while on a study abroad program. Hopefully, most of the contemplated changes will not be necessary, but the process of thinking about the possible need to change may better prepare an individual to change, if and when such changes are deemed appropriate.

Unfortunately, too often, individuals only think about behavioral options when there is a crisis. While some people are very good in responding to a crisis in their lives, most people by nature are not prone to be as effective when things are coming at them rapidly without much time to objectively and strategically think through possible options. Since change of one sort or another will be inevitable, being prepared beforehand is a very good place to be if the contemplated situation happens.

The third step is to realize that the more you are prepared to be flexible in adjusting to change, the better prepared you will be with options. Fewer options will mean fewer potential choices that can be effective to deal with the situations. Think in terms of you having to change your thinking or behaviors, rather than the other way where others are expected to change their thinking or behaviors to better suit you or that the unfavorable status quo will adjust to your preferences.

In summary, a meaningful study abroad experience requires changes. Maybe the biggest change that occurs will be in the personal growth of one's perspective of life and in discovery of new ways to adapt and cope to meet new challenges. It is very important to first recognize and accept that change will be inevitable. Make no mistake about it–a significant part of the experience of studying abroad is the realization that change will be required of you.

"Nothing is worse than missing an opportunity that could have changed your life."

CIRCUMSTANCES AND OPPORTUNITIES

As one gets older in age, most individuals have a tendency to look back on life and review what could have, might have, or even would have happened if different choices were made when certain favorable circumstances and opportunities were available. Usually at the point of the review, the potential opportunities are long gone and one is oftentimes left with a feeling of regret for not taking advantage of the lost opportunities.

Most of us have these "could have, should have, would have" regrets and we really don't know if a different choice would have produced a more favorable outcome to one's life, but we know that our life's path would have definitely been very different. And it is human nature to continue this second-guessing until we die.

Opportunities are often very time specific and they can occur by happenstance or through planned actions. They are, however, usually very fleeting and if not taken when presented, their "shelf life" expires and other opportunities and distractions may take their place. Studying abroad is one such opportunity for high school graduates and university students. It can occur when one considers options for a more challenging and experiential type of learning upon graduating from high school.

If one is serious about availing him/herself of the study abroad opportunity, there are some minimum considerations that can be very helpful in making the experience as successful as possible. For those who are still willing to consider the opportunity of studying abroad for a degree, the time to give greater consideration to the option is a couple of years before graduating from high school.

While studying abroad cannot be for everyone due to a lack of financial resources, or an individual's prior academic achievements are not good enough to gain admission, or family circumstances prevents one from furthering one's education, or a host of other legitimate reasons, there are also still a large number of students who intend to go on to an institution of higher learning after completion of their high school education. These types of students are the potential audience for which this book focuses its attention.

Making a decision to go on a study abroad program should not take place on a spur of the moment in a person's last year in high school because while there are many benefits to studying abroad, there are also many things to consider in making a decision which is right for each individual. Obviously, one is going to try to select the most appropriate institution and environment in the US and its experiences and commitment to foreign students. Another is an objective examination of one's expectations, temperament, and personality preferences when faced with challenges and adversity.

One of the best ways to conduct this latter type of analysis, other than taking a pencil and paper and conducting a personality/style preference inventory, would be to ask those who know you quite well and who are willing to be candid in their own assessment of a) how you tend to relate to other people, including complete strangers; b) coping mechanisms you have exhibited when facing new and challenging situations; and c) your chances of being sufficiently independent to survive and thrive in an environment where one has to establish new support systems, including environments where there are only a few or no students from one's native country.

CIRCUMSTANCES AND OPPORTUNITIES

If you do not seem to match up well with what may be required during a study abroad experience, then going overseas for a higher education experience may not be suitable for you. As stated earlier, study abroad may not be a good fit for everyone, but for those who can meet the challenges successfully, the opportunity will be well worth the effort.

In addition to the preparation which will be necessary prior to actually going on a study abroad program, it would be very helpful prior to departing one's native country to have a written plan as to how one can maximize the potential personal development and growth experiences in another country. The plan is to deliberately and consciously create as many opportunities for oneself because there is no better teacher than first-hand experience.

Without a plan, foreign students tend to struggle because there are no short or long-term strategies to overcome many of the challenges they will face while studying abroad. Without a plan, students tend to let situations and circumstances dictate their options and positively or negatively impact the study abroad experiences. That seems like more of a "hit" or "miss" approach and is too dependent upon luck and circumstances.

That is why it will be very helpful to have a personal growth plan that tends to create new learning opportunities for the individual to increase the comfort level in the years spent studying abroad. It can begin with relatively low risk, more easily attainable goals and once achieved, one is more prepared to take on more high risk experiences which require a greater level of confidence and represent new challenges for the individual.

If the strategy is to improve one's proficiency of the English language, the plan could call for making an effort to speak to as many people as possible utilizing the English language. The plan could be to start out practicing one's English with a small circle of acquaintances who have a little better proficiency of the English language and who are willing

CIRCUMSTANCES AND OPPORTUNITIES

to provide one with feedback on his/her endeavors. It is advisable for an individual to not try to end up practicing English with other foreign students whose proficiency of English would be considered below your own level of proficiency.

The reason is that there is usually a tendency of people to drop down to the minimum standard level so your English skills may not necessarily improve over time. Furthermore, while these individuals may be willing to provide you with feedback, their proficiency in English may not compel you to expand your vocabulary and better understand the subtle nuances of the English language.

Without a deliberate plan of improvement, you may find that after a number of months/years studying in the US, your English proficiency is relatively close to the level when you first entered the program. It would be sad if this happened because, most likely, you did not have a conscious written plan to improve your English proficiency. The world of possibilities to create new circumstances and opportunities can be limitless if they are properly planned.

Even if the first task or activity doesn't produce the desired result, after objective evaluation of what worked and what didn't work, one should be better prepared to try the same task or activity again. Hopefully, this time the task or activity will be more successful because more thought has gone into the preparation.

Without a deliberate plan, there is too much that will be left to chance. It's like eating new foods. Initially, there is possible reluctance to trying something different from what one is accustomed to eating. However, especially if one likes the new food, it gets easier to try other similar types of food because of the relative comfort level and success with the initial experience. Conversely, if the initial experience in eating new food is not very pleasant, there is a greater reluctance to not try other new foods because of the first experience.

Nevertheless, if one only uses the unpleasant experience as the primary reason for not wanting to try new foods, the individual will potentially be missing out on tasting foods that he/she would really like if one had tried it. That is similar to study abroad experiences. Initial success will lead to a greater comfort level to try again, while unpleasant experiences will tend to be obstacles to going down that road again.

One of the major reasons for studying abroad is to have new experiences and to learn from the experiences, whether they are successful or not. The more an individual tries new things, the greater the likelihood of expanding his/her knowledge base to successfully handle new, first-time experiences.

Once the study abroad experience is over, many have regrets that there were too many missed opportunities of new experiences and lost chances to challenge oneself. In order to reduce the level of regret, the time to experiment and push oneself is during the study abroad college years because after that, as most young adults mature into full adulthood, "life happens." This means that you have to become more responsible, get a job, work, and maybe get married and start a family. There won't be any more chances to complete what you had the chance to do in the US.

> *"Nothing great in the world has ever been accomplished without passion."*
>
> -Georg Wilhelm Friedrich Hegel-

FIND YOUR LIFE PASSION AND PURPOSE

Studying abroad in the US will give you so many opportunities to discover what and how other students from the US and other countries think and to see what they aspire to be and do with their lives. It offers and exposes you to possibilities and perspectives that you potentially would never have experienced in your home country. You will also learn what true freedom is and you may also reflect upon whether total freedom is actually healthy or not for a society and the individual.

Remember that sometimes a positive idea or concept taken to an extreme can sometimes turn into a negative. You will experience struggles and adversity, but through your strength and determination to never give up, you will grow and eventually reach a level of self-confidence that only an experience like studying abroad can give you. And through all your study abroad trials and hardships, discussions, fun and enjoyment, you, hopefully, will find what your life's passion, your life's purpose is all about.

For some of you, it will be to return to work in business in your home country to help local businesses become more competitive, efficient, effective, and vibrant in the 21st century. For others, it may be to continue in graduate school in the US, or maybe to try to get a job working in the US or another country outside of the US. Still others may want to become a teacher or an entrepreneur. When you are a university student in the US, all of life possibilities and dreams are on the table.

FIND YOUR LIFE PASSION AND PURPOSE

That is what a study abroad opportunity in the US can offer you. It can expose you to the limitless possibilities of what you can do with your life and it can be the chance to discover your life passion and purpose. Because once we know what our life's passion is, the rest will start to fall into place.

The sad part for many people in the world, including many Americans, is that they never find their true life passion. They often continue their lives focused on trying to earn enough for a satisfactory life and working at making that happen, but they are not excited about their job or what they do. They tend to become too comfortable with the status quo and while the job may not be ideal, they tend to rationalize that it is "not so bad." And this is the "mediocrity trap" that keeps them in the same job and position for years.

As people get older, they become more afraid of the unknown and they usually decide to play it safe instead of following their long-lost dreams and goals. I believe there is a big difference between "existing" and "living." People who are just existing are not following their life's passion or purpose. I feel sorry for these people and that is why I am very excited for all of you who will have study abroad opportunities in the US. It will open up worlds and unexpected advantages that you never dreamed existed.

Even in my case, I have always been passionate about life but did not find my true life's passion for many years. But I was passionate to find my life's passion, if that makes sense. I never gave up looking for it, but it took me over 30 years to find my life's passion. It was always just beyond my reach. But because of all my experiences on study abroad programs and working in international education, I was finally able to find my life's passion and purpose – and that is you!

My life passion is to inspire and encourage foreign students to study abroad in the US because like it was for me, study abroad will be a life-changing experience for you. It should open doors that will help you find your life's passion or at least give you the skills and tools to keep you striving to find your life's passion or purpose.

And once you find it, everything else will start to fall into place because you know where you are going and what needs to be done. The road map to reach your goals becomes very clear. And that is one of the biggest opportunities that study abroad in the US will offer you.

I have always believed that life is too short. And when the end appears to be approaching, the last thing you want to have are regrets. We will all naturally have some personal regrets, but the ideal is to have as few of them as possible. Don't let a missed opportunity to study abroad haunt you as a regret for the rest of your life. In the profound words of Katherine Gascoigne, "Make it a rule of life never to regret and never to look back." Just do it!

"I am not an Athenian or a Greek, but a citizen of the world."

-Socrates-

THE GLOBAL CITIZEN

In Japan, the government's new initiative is for Japanese students to have overseas study abroad experiences so they can become Japan's global human resources in the future. The government's vision for the future citizens of Japan is that they will be part of a diverse workforce, working with others from different cultures and countries, communicating effectively in English, competing internationally, and doing business outside of Japan.

In short, the Japanese government wants international Japanese "work warriors" to help Japan compete globally throughout the world. Although this is important for the country, I don't believe that this is necessarily what is in the best interest of the individual.

What I hope happens is that many foreign students will aspire to become "Global Citizens" who have the ability to work globally in other countries and with people from other cultures. But I believe there are more worthy and visionary outcomes of study abroad programs that are just as important. And that is the ability to demonstrate intercultural empathy and competence, to be a visionary, to be able to think big and accomplish lofty ideas, to have a charitable and compassionate heart, and to be able to do the right thing, which is not always the same as doing things right.

Being a "Global Citizen" starts with a mindset, an attitude, that can then lead to behaviors which are reflective of this commitment. Without such a frame of mind, it is a struggle to constantly remind oneself of the responsibilities and obligations of being more than just a citizen of one's home country.

The irony of the Japanese perspective is what appears to be a lack of understanding where the interdependence of today's world requires a shift in thinking from "old world" theories and practices to the realities of the future. For many years, countries could become economic global leaders by coming up with new ideas or practices which made that country stand out from the rest of the world.

For instance, the US became the leader of the mass market movement after World War II as other countries tried to replicate similar results. Japan took the lead in the 1980s with its superior quality productivity models and China is the current front runner in the twenty-first century. All of these efforts were predicated on a country being somewhat independent of what was taking place elsewhere. Competition was the driver in each country's efforts to outdo the competition and/or come up with a better business model for success.

THE GLOBAL CITIZEN

Much has changed over the past seventy years as the world has literally gotten smaller and there is far greater interdependence between countries and geographic regions. No longer are problems or successes in one country or region immune from having a world-wide impact. With the internet and social media, no longer is it sufficient to think only of the impact of one country's behavior to the exclusion of neighboring countries, regions, or the world.

As a result of the far greater interdependence of countries or regions, one needs to begin seriously thinking about the global state of affairs, implications, and opportunities. What was previously more localized in a country now has greater applications and implications that could impact the entire world. Consequently, the thinking that emphasized national or regional implications should be expanded in the future to give greater emphasis on the implications for the rest of the world.

However, like the saying "politics start locally," it is crucial that one takes this frame of mind and applies it first to the country where one comes from. Being a "Global Citizen" first begins where one originates from because both physically and attitudinally, it is easier to behave accordingly when the characteristics can be practically and meaningfully applied to everyday life. It may be asking too much for people to become "Global Citizens" when they have difficulty applying it as part of their daily life or to even begin thinking about social and political implications elsewhere. Extending the concepts of being a "Global Citizen" to the larger world one lives in may be impossible when one does not practice and apply the concepts into situations in one's home country where one theoretically has more control on a day-to-day basis.

A global citizen is one that I believe can see the problems and struggles of the world, can feel the pain and hardship of those who are in terrible situations, and can lift and inspire people to reach their potential and be successful. This is my ideal of who the "Global Citizen" is. I hope everyone will eventually reach beyond just being a global human resource or a working international warrior and can reach the renaissance level of being a "Global Citizen."

As the Greek philosopher Socrates proclaimed over 2,400 years ago "I am not an Athenian or a Greek, but a citizen of the world." This attitude is more necessary today than ever before if we are to make a difference in a much more complex, complicated, and interdependent world than existed during Socrates' life.

Experience is the teacher of all things.
                                    -Julius Caesar-

IT IS ALL UP TO YOU!

I have elaborated on the benefits, skills, and overall gains of a study abroad experience to the US. But none of what was written can happen unless you make the effort. You must remember that going to classes and getting good grades are the basic minimum requirements to success in studying abroad. But it will take more than just these minimal requirements to optimize and maximize the study abroad experience.

Ideally, for the experience to become a significantly meaningful and life-changing one, you will need to completely immerse yourself in student and campus life, as well as the community off campus. This requires you to leave your comfort zone and meet as many people as you can. You can start by leaving your dormitory room, then venturing out of your dormitory, and finally going beyond the campus.

You need to consciously make an effort to meet and talk to different people on campus and at the dining facilities, join campus clubs to expand your circle of friends, attend various sessions with guest speakers on new topics beyond your current interests, go out and watch movies and plays, participate in intramural sports opportunities or join university sports teams, support and watch school sports events, volunteer your time to worthwhile causes, go hiking and biking or kayaking, and see the community and surrounding area.

In short, unless you take the initiative and encounter risks and experiences beyond classes and studies, get involved on campus and with community activities and events, you could return to your home country with the very minimum of experiences and miss out on the other essential 50% of the study abroad experience.

The study abroad experience framework is all set up for you, the "players" are all on "stage," but if you do not engage and take advantage of what is there for the taking and learning, then you are potentially the only one to lose out by not pushing yourself out of your comfort zone. If you are somewhat uncomfortable about attending campus activities and events on your own, to feel more comfortable ask friends or roommates to join you as you venture out into new experiences and settings.

While there is no sure-fire guarantee for success on any study abroad program, I believe that the first and most important thing is to get involved and make friends. We have a couple of sayings in America that I hope you will keep in mind. One common saying is "Nothing ventured, nothing gained." This means that if you don't try something new, you are apt not to experience or learn anything new. The other saying is to "Hit the ground running." This means that from the moment you step onto campus, you should be ready and prepared to positively assert yourself, get involved and be ready with a smile to greet and say "hello" to as many people in your dorm and on campus whom you meet, and offer a hand to others if they need help moving into their dorm room or carrying boxes somewhere. That is one of the best ways to meet other students, offer to assist or help them carry or move something.

Also take immediate action on all of the things that you will need to do. Do not procrastinate because there may not be enough time to do everything and procrastinating has the potential of rushing you into doing things at the last minute so you forget about the attention to details which potentially can become a big problem later if not addressed promptly.

Don't put something off and say something like, "I will do it tomorrow or next week when I feel like it." Always remember, "Action doesn't follow feeling, feeling follows action." So if you have to, "Fake it, until you make it."

If you are bored on campus or have no friends or are still homesick or experiencing culture shock after 1-2 months after arriving in the US, then the cause of the problem is most likely a result of your actions and behavior, or more accurately, the lack of actions and active behaviors. The cause of the problem is probably not the university or the location of the school. Based on my many years of involvement and experience with study abroad programs, the problem would most likely be your reluctance or resistance to take a risk, be assertive, or opening yourself up to campus and student life.

You have to realize that you will only get back what you put into it. It's an investment. You have to put something out to get something back. Consequently, if you put in zero effort to get out of your dorm room and be involved, then you should expect zero back in return. In short, it is completely up to YOU!

Study abroad is not for everyone, nor will everyone have the required time, finances, and personal commitment needed to maximize the effort.

Nevertheless, individuals willing to take the risk and leave their comfort zone will be on the right path to being successful on study abroad. And if you follow what has been written in this book to better prepare yourself before and after you arrive on campus, I am certain that you will have a much greater chance of having an unforgettable and very successful study abroad experience in the US.

Be forewarned that the person who completes a study abroad program will be a far different person than the one who first arrived on campus. You will discover that you have grown and matured through new experiences that have challenged your values, beliefs, and perspectives of your country, culture and world.

PREPARATION CHECKLIST

Before you leave your home country for your study abroad opportunity in the US, here are some things that you may want to do in advance to better help prepare yourself for your study abroad experience:

1) Work on your oral and writing English language skills. Find a native English language exchange partner or someone in a nearby location who is proficient in the English language or you could attend an English language school, but try to be sure to practice with and learn from people who are native or proficient English speakers.

Native English speakers will help you expand your vocabulary of English words as well as helping you learn to use "living" English words or phrases which includes slangs, popular expressions, and metaphors. You should also work on conversing at a comparable speed used in everyday American conversations.

PREPARATION CHECKLIST

Written English will also be essential for when you study in the US. There are many papers and reports to write, as well as some final exams will involve essay questions where your written responses must be clear and concise.

It would also be very helpful if you can read newspapers, magazines, novels, and books printed in English. Doing so will increase your vocabulary and help with your understanding of English sentence structure, as well as prepare you to read faster and increase your comprehension for when you are in classes in the US.

2) Be knowledgeable about current events taking place in the world and in the US. In order to be part of the discussion and part of the conversation with classmates and friends, you will need to be up to date on world and current events. Also some of the other topics of discussion to become familiar with should include but not be limited to the basics in such topics as economics, religion, political ideology, social issues, and philosophy.

3) Be knowledgeable about the history of the US and what has transpired throughout the 250 year history of the country. Pay special attention to civil rights and racial equality, from slavery to the civil rights movement, including what is happening in the US today with the "Black Lives Matter" movement. Be aware of what is happening in the US politically with the election of Donald Trump.

4) Be knowledgeable about your home country's culture and history and how it has shaped foreign policy within the region, with the US, and the world. You should be prepared to explain in clear and logical English when speaking or writing about any issues regarding your country.

5) Be aware of the stereotypes and images of your country that Americans may hold. This will help you when people ask you questions that may seem rude or ignorant. Remember, don't get upset or mad if people say things that are not true about your country. You will find that

most of the time, people just don't know any better. It may be due to a basic lack of knowledge where their comments may sometimes appear to border on ignorance or naivety.

6) Practice doing presentations in front of people, even if it is in your home country language. The main thing is that you start getting used to talking in front of people. Try to speak in a very inspiring way. My suggestion would be to start out with topics that you know very well and can easily talk about. You will be much more passionate and confident to speak about something you know very well or are familiar with.

7) Be able to use the Microsoft Office programs on a computer such as Power Point, Excel, and Word. These are the minimum software programs that you should know and if you don't, be sure to learn how to use these software programs before you leave for the US. The time you have to spend on learning a new software program in the US will take away valuable time which you could devote to studies and experiencing life on campus.

8) Begin researching websites of possible US universities and colleges that you may want to attend. Look for the admission requirements, costs, location, student services for foreign students, and dormitory space. Make a pros and cons chart and start comparing schools which are on your "wish list." I also host a study abroad web page where I recommend certain universities that I believe have an all-around, complete package for international students. They are not necessarily ranked universities but will offer you a very good education and good value in the US. If you are interested, please check the website: Goglobal.me

9) Learn as much as you can about different social media. Once you arrive in the US, you can use different platforms and social media with different international students. Different countries use different platforms. For example, in Thailand and Japan they tend to use Line. WeChat and QQ are used in China. Facebook and Twitter (both banned in China) are

PREPARATION CHECKLIST

the two big players throughout the world. Presently for young millennials in the US, the two most popular social media seem to be Snapchat and Instagram. As you well know, social media is constantly changing and evolving. So, learn as much as you can about different social media platforms so you can experiment and use them in the US. Social media will only keep growing and has so much potential for future businesses and ideas. And it will help you keep in touch with all of your international friends.

Other considerations to possibly add to your checklist might include:
- Checking into student visa (or other entry) requirements, especially deadlines for application and receiving the documents well in advance of traveling to the US.
- Checking into the application rate versus the actual foreign student acceptance rate of various institutions to get a more realistic expectation of possibilities, rather than thinking that all institutions' acceptance rates are relatively equal.
- Understanding the US monetary system, the applicable conversion rates, and the financial impact for however long a student plans to study abroad.
- Becoming more familiar with the respective institution's degree or graduation requirements, credit transfer process and criteria for acceptance, dropping and retaking courses, GPA requirements, etc.
- Emphasizing the need to stay ahead of the institutional requirements, deadlines, and policies and other foreign students whom one is technically competing against for entry at an institution, on-campus jobs, etc.

CONCLUSION: YOU WILL NEVER BE THE SAME!

No other experience will help an individual mature and grow as much as a study abroad experience. Many times the growth occurs as a result of the struggles and hardships, not necessarily from the happy and more enjoyable times. And often an individual will not realize how much he/she has been touched or affected by the study abroad experience until he/she has returned back to one's home country. Only then will the individual start to decompress because during the study abroad experience, he/she had so much input and exposure to new information and experiences that the person did not have enough time to reflect and make sense of the experiences.

After returning home, it can take up to 3-6 months to be able to make some sense of what had just been experienced in the US and how everything can potentially be used from all the new knowledge acquired and experiences encountered to enhance a person's career and future. Some graduates will experience "reverse culture shock," which is the opposite of culture shock. It happens sometimes when study abroad students return home and they find that their lives and views of the world have changed so significantly while everyone back home remained the same as when the person first left to study abroad.

For some returning students, it could be quite frustrating and depressing, but it is also important to understand and realize that those who remained back did not have the opportunity to see a totally different world and eye-opening perspectives. It is critically important for graduates of study abroad programs not to be condescending of those who did not have the same opportunities, but to make the most of what they have learned and to figure out how to apply it to their future. Also these graduates can become positive role models and encourage others at home to study abroad in the US.

A study abroad experience is priceless and no one can ever take it away from you. It is an experience that will give a person unforgettable lifetime memories and friends from all over the world. In addition to having new friends and acquaintances, many study abroad participants will have the opportunity to create new networks and future business contacts from all parts of the globe.

Studying abroad also gives an individual the opportunity to see all of the good and bad in one's home country. It may not be so black and white as one now looks at the world through a different set of lenses. Likewise, one cannot help but also see the good and the bad of things in the US. My honest hope is that you will keep the good things and meaningful values from your home country, as well as also bring home the good ideas and effective ways of thinking from the US. Hopefully, you will become a kind of "global hybrid," with the best of both worlds. And this is what the global citizen represents. Taking the best from different countries and cultures and reinventing one's self to become an eclectic person who will bring positive change to the world.

Study abroad opportunities offer an individual the chance to understand one's identity and how that individual relates to his/her ethnic heritage, as well as helping an individual define the core values that he/she wants to keep which will guide the person for the rest of his/her life. For some study abroad students, they will find out that they really belong back home and want to return and stay in their native country after graduation. This is fine because while they were studying abroad, they may have learned and realized about the really good things that their home country has and represents and that home was the best place for them. Others will want to reinvent themselves and take certain good values and practices

CONCLUSION: YOU WILL NEVER BE THE SAME!

from different countries and mold themselves into a global citizen. Every student will take home something different from the study abroad experience. All one can do is do his/her personal best and see where the study abroad experience can take the individual in the future.

To be able to maximize the benefits of studying abroad, one must experience it personally. It is not something that can be learned secondhand or through other people's experiences or vicariously. The opportunity to live it, to experiment with its various challenges, and to face new forms of adversity all contribute to an individual's personal growth which a person will undergo in a relatively short period of his/her lifetime. There will be very few opportunities of this magnitude which have the potential of reshaping an individual's life for the future. The time, money, and commitment an individual is willing to give for a study abroad experience will someday probably prove to be the best investment a person could ever make in his/her personal growth and life.

I hope that if there is a chance for you to study abroad, that you will take advantage of the opportunity because the opportunity is not available to everyone. Only those knowledgeable of the depth of the experience, coupled with the financial and time requirements, will ever have the opportunity to take advantage of the immense value of studying abroad. Ironically, it may be years later that you look back at the study abroad experience and start to fathom objectively how important and valuable those experiences were and how they have shaped the rest of your life.

Study abroad opportunities offer an individual the ideal platform for "autonomy, mastery and purpose." And these three ideas are the path to greater lifelong happiness. I really hope this book can help you in some way as I am a true believer in the power of study abroad experiences and all the benefits, skills, struggles, and growth that come with it.

CONCLUSION: YOU WILL NEVER BE THE SAME!

If you have any questions or if you would like more information on possible US universities to consider, please email me and/or check the website: Goglobal.me

Thank you,

Mike Matsuno
Email: mikematsuno@mac.com
Website for more information: Goglobal.me

CLOSING COMMENTS

I would like to close by reminding everyone that what I have written in this book is not set in stone and will not be the same for every university or college or region. With 4,000 institutions of higher education in the US, there are so many different application requirements and systems, financial costs and fees, and university student systems. So please check on the websites of the universities that you plan to apply to and confirm all the important information directly with them. There is no one set manual that encompasses everything that an individual will need to know and do when applying or attending US universities. This book is a good starting point for those possibly interested in studying abroad as it covers a wide range of considerations that are not institution-specific. Once an individual has determined that he/she will more earnestly pursue the option of studying abroad, there are many other institution-specific books and websites that go into more detail about the actual application process and student visa requirements. Please look to these books or the websites of the universities for this type of assistance and for the most updated information.

This book was written to focus on what I call "Global Success Skills," which many today refer to as "soft skills" which are necessary for ensuring success in study abroad opportunities. I believe that "soft skills" are just as important as "hard skills" which can be defined and measured like math, writing, a degree, speaking a foreign language, etc. Consequently, "soft skills" tend to focus on the important areas of personal development and growth that should be given careful thought and reflection throughout the study abroad experience because they are generally the key factors which determine how to ultimately achieve success.

WITH SINCERE APPRECIATION

I would like to sincerely thank Nelson Okino for all of his valuable time and tireless effort to help me with the main editing of this book. This book could not have been completed without his help. And I would also like to thank Stella Maxwell for her continued support and encouragement to complete this book. Lastly, my deepest thanks to all of the students, parents and young people who I have met in the last 25 years who have given me the chance to find my passion which has been to inspire and encourage young people from all over the world to study abroad for a life-changing experience!

ABOUT THE AUTHOR

Mike Matsuno was raised in Honolulu, Hawaii and is a 4th generation, Japanese American. His great grandparents immigrated from Japan to Hawaii over 120 years ago. Mike's parents being of the third generation (sansei) did not speak any Japanese and the Matsuno Family only spoke English. In his junior year at Willamette University in Salem, Oregon, Mike enrolled in a one-semester study abroad program to Japan to study Japanese and Japanese culture. That one semester abroad would forever change his life.

Since his first study abroad experience, Mike has been on seven other study abroad programs to Guatemala, Indonesia, Laos, and four other separate study abroad programs to Japan. He has two master's degrees, he studied at the University of Hawaii at Manoa, and then studied at Doshisha University in Kyoto in Japanese. He also taught as a faculty member at both American and Japanese universities in both English and Japanese and he has been working in international education for the last 25 years.

He taught six years at the University of Alaska Fairbanks and was responsible for the selection, preparation and management of the outbound Japan exchange program which sent American students to Japan for study abroad opportunities. He then moved to Japan where he was the Director of the International Center at Osaka Gakuin University for 10 years. He was in charge of all areas of study abroad opportunities, student exchanges, and international education-related programs. For the last two years, Mike has worked for California State University Monterey Bay (CSUMB) as its international consultant and recruiter in charge of university partnerships and Asian student recruitment. He is presently doing consulting for Haddington International Education (HIE) based

ABOUT THE AUTHOR

in Dublin, Ireland (http://www.hie.ie) and is also working with the Japan Study Abroad Foundation (JSAF) located in Tokyo, Japan (http://www.japanstudyabroad.org).

NOTES

Maslow's Hierarchy of Needs. http://www.deepermind.com/20maslow.htm

Sammy Takahashi, former owner and President of Pacific Gateway International College in Vancouver, Canada. Graduate of CSU Fresno, California. Originally from Japan and presently living in Vancouver, Canada.

Dale Carnegie, *How to Win Friends and Influence People*. 1936. https://en.wikipedia.org/wiki/How_to_Win_Friends_and_Influence_People

Daniel Pink: *The Puzzle of Motivation*. Ted Talks. He speaks about autonomy, mastery and purpose. http://www.ted.com/talks/dan_pink_on_motivation#t-748437

Nobuyuki Suzuki: President and CEO, Estrellita Co., Ltd. Consultant, career counseling for Japanese students who participated on study abroad and/or worked overseas. https://www.linkedin.com/in/nobuyuki-suzuki-1885b921/

Google's Eight Innovation Principles: #5 Never fail to fail. The importance of rapid iteration: "Fail frequently, Fail fast, and fail forward." From the book, *Bold*. **Peter H. Diamonds and Steven Kotler**. http://www.simonandschuster.com/books/Bold/Peter-H-Diamandis/9781476709581

Thomas Boswell, *The Heart of the Order*. 1989. https://www.tavbooks.com/pages/books/15503.1/baseball-thomas-boswell/the-heart-of-the-order

Printed in Poland
by Amazon Fulfillment
Poland Sp. z o.o., Wrocław